ELECTION MANIPULATION:

Is America's Voting System Secure?

John Allen

ReferencePoint Press

San Diego, CA

ReferencePoint Press®

For more information, contact:
ReferencePoint Press, Inc.
PO Box 27779
San Diego, CA 92198
www.ReferencePointPress.com

LIBRARY OF CONGRESS CATALOGING-IN-PUBLICATION DATA

Name: Allen, John, 1957– author.
Title: Election Manipulation: Is America's Voting System Secure?/John Allen.
Description: San Diego, CA: ReferencePoint Press, 2020. |
Includes bibliographical references and index.
Identifiers: LCCN 2019042848 | ISBN
9781682828076 (library binding) | ISBN 9781682828083 (ebook)
Subjects: Juvenile literature.

CONTENTS

A Stern Warning

On July 24, 2019, special prosecutor Robert Mueller made a highly anticipated appearance on Capitol Hill. Before two committees in Congress, Mueller answered questions about his team's recent probe into Russian interference in the 2016 presidential election. The nearly two-year investigation found numerous instances of Russian meddling in the election, many of which led to indictments. Russia had interfered in two ways—first, by carrying out a social media campaign that favored the Republican candidate, Donald Trump; second, by hacking into the computer networks of Hillary Clinton's campaign and the Democratic National Committee (DNC).

In the end, Mueller's team determined there was insufficient evidence that Trump or members of his campaign had conspired with Russians in these activities. The team reached no conclusion as to whether Trump had acted to obstruct the investigation. During hours of testimony, Mueller added little to the official report on the probe. However, when asked whether Russia might be planning attacks on future US elections, the former FBI director delivered a stern warning. "It wasn't a single attempt," he said. "They're doing it as we sit here."[1]

Faith in the Integrity of Elections

The Mueller Report's revelations about Russian interference sent shock waves through the halls of Congress and the nation. One day after Mueller's testimony, there was more evidence of Russian mischief. The Senate Intelligence Committee released a report claiming that in 2016 Russia had targeted election systems in all fifty states. The report contends that federal officials underestimated Russia's drive to interfere in the election. As a result, state officials received inadequate warnings and did not react strongly enough.

> **"It wasn't a single attempt. They're doing it as we sit here."[1]**
>
> —Special prosecutor Robert Mueller on Russian interference in US elections

In a democracy that prides itself on free and fair elections, it is vital that American citizens not lose faith in the integrity of the election process. With its attempts to meddle in US elections, Russia seeks to destroy that faith. Beyond supporting individual candidates, Russian hackers want to spread confusion and discord among Americans. In April 2019, soon after the release of the Mueller Report, FBI director Christopher Wray warned that Russia's attacks would not wait for 2020 but were ongoing. "What has pretty much continued unabated is the use of social media, fake news, propaganda, false personas, etc. to spin us up, pit us against each other, to sow divisiveness and discord, to undermine America's faith in democracy," Wray said. "That is not just an election-cycle threat. It is pretty much a 365-day-a-year threat."[2] In response, Wray announced that the FBI was enlisting agents and analysts to bolster America's defenses against election interference.

Wray's boss in the White House has not been so forthright in his rhetoric. Trump believes that the focus on Russia's meddling in the election is really an attempt to question the legitimacy of his victory. At joint press events with Russian president Vladimir Putin, Trump has accepted Putin's claims that there was no interference. However, eight federal and congressional intelligence and national security groups, from the CIA to the House and Senate Intelligence Committees, have concluded that Russia interfered in the 2016 election.

Special prosecutor Robert Mueller meets with the House Judiciary Committee in July of 2019. Mueller answered questions about his team's probe into Russian interference in the 2016 presidential election.

Warnings About Election Attacks in 2020

US law enforcement and intelligence agencies are already warning about likely attempts to interfere in the 2020 election as well. Officials see Russia, with its sophisticated tools for cyberattack and propaganda, as the most urgent ongoing threat. But they also believe other foreign countries and domestic groups may try to manipulate the election. In response, certain federal agencies, including the National Security Agency and the US Cyber Command, have expanded and formed a joint task force to combat Russian influence in the months leading up to the election.

Officials are focused on three main methods of attack. The first is hacking into computer networks run by political parties or campaigns. If hackers gain access to these systems, they can steal information about campaign strategies, polling, and opposition research. Armed with this information, hackers could spoil campaign plans by publishing them online or reveal the methods used to gather dirt on political opponents. They can also arrange for stolen emails to be made public, as was done by Russian hackers in the run-up to the 2016 election. Emails hacked from the DNC led to embarrassing revelations about the inner workings of the campaign.

Another method is using social media to spread false or misleading information. Political ads on Facebook or Instagram can influence voters with inflammatory attacks on candidates or deceptive takes on social issues. Fake news stories from obscure websites can be posted on Twitter and then retweeted thousands of times. Sizable numbers of readers may accept them as true before they can be debunked by respectable news sources.

A third method is tampering with the voting process itself, including the vote count. Hackers can break into election board computers and tamper with voter registration data. Some fear that electronic voting machines could be manipulated by hackers or tampered with on-site. Hackers also could interfere with how votes are counted and how the totals are reported.

Approaching the Threat with Urgency

All of these methods—along with whatever new techniques might be in the works—are apt to erode Americans' confidence in their democracy. Experts say federal and state governments must approach the threat with more urgency. Better communication is needed to warn campaigns and election officials when hacking is detected. Social media companies must take steps to eliminate fake news and deceptive ads. More money must be spent to shore up the nation's voting system. "Election security is national security," says Elizabeth Howard, former deputy commissioner for the Virginia Department of Elections, "and we are only as strong as our weakest link."[3]

"Election security is national security, and we are only as strong as our weakest link."[3]

—Elizabeth Howard, former deputy commissioner for the Virginia Department of Elections

CHAPTER ONE

Hacking into Campaign Networks

Microsoft, one of the world's leading technology companies, knows a hacking scheme when it sees one. The company spends vast sums to protect its software from malicious hackers. And long before American voters go to the polls in November 2020, cybersecurity experts at Microsoft are already warning of foreign attempts to hack into the computer systems of campaigns and related political groups.

In July 2019 Microsoft announced that its threat intelligence team had detected Russian hackers at work against United States think tanks, academic groups, and nongovernmental organizations. These are groups that help political campaigns prepare strategy and address current issues. The hackers include Russian cybercriminals known as Fancy Bear. Prior to the 2016 presidential election, they managed to break into the computer networks of Hillary Clinton's campaign and the DNC. Experts at Microsoft are all but certain that Fancy Bear is preparing another round of attacks for the run-up to the 2020 election. Moreover, they fear that campaigns are still vulnerable. According to Tom Burt, Microsoft's vice president of customer security and trust, "Many organizations essential to democracy do not have the resources or expertise to defend themselves against cyberattacks."[4]

Probing for Weaknesses

Hackers seem to be probing for weaknesses in preparation for the 2020 presidential campaign. Burt says Microsoft's threat intelligence team has uncovered hacking attacks against various targets in the past two years. In 2018 Microsoft alerted more than ten thousand customers to attacks from Russia, North Korea, and Iran, most of them aimed at corporations or political groups. In the months before the 2018 midterm elections in the United States, Fancy Bear hackers set up fake Internet domains linked to two conservative nonprofit groups. One was the Hudson Institute, a prominent think tank. The other was the International Republican Institute, whose board of directors includes six Republican senators. Microsoft acted quickly to notify the organizations about the threats.

> "Many organizations essential to democracy do not have the resources or expertise to defend themselves against cyberattacks."[4]
>
> —Tom Burt, Microsoft's vice president of customer security and trust

According to analysts at the security firm FireEye, Fancy Bear has also targeted campaigns in the 2019 parliamentary elections in Europe. Campaign workers in several European Union countries received emails with fake links to government websites. The links could allow hackers to get access to the campaigns' computer systems. It is unclear whether sensitive data was leaked, but FireEye notes that this type of hacking is usually successful. "It's clear that democracies around the world are under attack," says Brad Smith, Microsoft's president and chief legal officer.

> Foreign entities are launching cyber strikes to disrupt elections and sow discord. Unfortunately, the internet has become an avenue for some governments to steal and leak information, spread disinformation, and probe and potentially attempt to tamper with voting systems.[5]

In response, tech firms have launched projects aimed at protecting political campaigns in the United States and the West. In 2017 Facebook contributed $500,000 to Harvard University's Kennedy School of Government to create an initiative called

Microsoft's threat intelligence team has uncovered hacking attacks against various targets in the past two years. In 2018 Microsoft alerted more than ten thousand customers to attacks, mostly toward corporations and political groups.

Defending Digital Democracy. One of its main goals is to help politicians and campaign personnel protect their networks from cyberattacks. In April 2018 Microsoft announced its own Defending Democracy Program, which includes measures for campaign security as well as tools to prevent disinformation and other online mischief. Diana Kelley, Microsoft's chief technology officer for cybersecurity, wants to advise campaigns on the various methods hackers use to infiltrate email accounts. "The first [goal] is to prevent the hacking, and to look at how they're hacking, what they're trying to accomplish,"[6] says Kelley. These tech-based programs are ramping up even more in anticipation of the 2020 campaign.

Russian Phishing Attacks

Experts warn that in 2020 hackers likely will try the approach that worked so well in the 2016 election: a basic cyberattack called phishing. In a phishing attack, a person receives an email containing a link or a password request. Clicking on the link or keying in the password enables hackers to infiltrate the computer system. According to the Mueller Report, military agents with the GPU, Russia's secret service, began their hacking efforts in March 2016. They used a special variation of phishing called spear phishing, in which fake emails seem to be from trusted sources, such as the government, banks, or tech companies.

The Russian hackers sent spear-phishing emails to various staff members on Clinton's campaign, including John Podesta, the campaign chair. Podesta received an email supposedly from Google claiming that a third party was trying to break into his account and urging him to change his password at once. An aide with access to Podesta's account saw the message and forwarded it to a staff

Bipartisan Hacking Attempts

Hackers also targeted the Republican National Committee (RNC) in 2016. In a January 2017 appearance before the Senate Intelligence Committee, then-FBI director James Comey said hackers believed to be Russians stole RNC emails. Comey revealed that the hacked RNC email domain was older and out of use. "There was evidence that there was hacking directed at state-level organizations and the RNC, but old domains of the RNC, that is, email domains they were no longer using," Comey told the committee. "Information was harvested from there, but it was old stuff. None of that was released." Comey added that he did not know whether hackers attempted to breach newer RNC emails or the Trump campaign. The fact that RNC emails went unpublished was one reason that intelligence officials determined Russia was intent on helping Donald Trump win the election.

Some cyber experts have expressed doubts about whether Russians actually hacked the DNC emails. Bill Binney, a retired technical director at the National Security Agency, believes the emails were downloaded to a thumb drive on-site at the DNC, perhaps by a staffer upset at the party's treatment of Bernie Sanders. Julian Assange, the founder of WikiLeaks, the site that published the stolen emails, has claimed the files did not come from the Russians. Robert Mueller did not have the DNC servers examined during his investigation, relying instead on information provided by Crowdstrike, a tech firm hired by the DNC. Mueller's team also did not interview Assange.

Quoted in Andy Greenberg, "Russia Hacked 'Older' Republican Emails, FBI Director Says," *Wired*, January 10, 2017. www.wired.com.

technician to see whether it was genuine. The technician recognized it as a hack attempt but replied with a fatal typo. He declared that the email was *legitimate*—not *illegitimate* as he intended—and advised Podesta to change his password immediately. When Podesta typed in the old password to make the change, Russian hackers gained access to thousands of Podesta's emails for the campaign.

Shortly thereafter, Russian GPU agents also used a spear-phishing ploy to hack into other networks, including those of the DNC and the Democratic Congressional Campaign Committee (DCCC). To divert investigators from their hacking scheme, the Russians masked themselves using an online persona, Guccifer 2.0. According to the Mueller Report, they passed thousands of stolen emails to WikiLeaks, an Internet site that specializes in publishing leaked or stolen materials. WikiLeaks released the emails and documents from Podesta and the DNC in stages prior to the November 2016 election. The release led to some embarrassing disclosures for Democrats and the Clinton campaign. For example, emails from the DNC showed that the committee had tried to undermine the campaign of Senator Bernie Sanders, Clinton's chief rival for the Democratic Party nomination.

Political analysts believe that some Sanders supporters, angered by the WikiLeaks emails, may have sat out the general election in protest or even voted for Trump. A survey of the 2016 presidential election by the Cooperative Congressional Election Study found that more than one in ten people who voted for Sanders in the Democratic primary switched to Trump in the general election. Political analysts note that there were many factors that led to Trump's surprising victory. But according to NPR political analyst Danielle Kurtzleben, "To answer the question that many Clinton supporters may be asking: . . . yes—there are enough of those Sanders-Trump voters [to] have potentially swung the election toward Clinton and away from Trump."[7]

Mueller and his team brought indictments against twelve Russian intelligence agents for their hacking activities. The Mueller Re-

Russian hackers targeted Hillary Clinton (pictured) during her 2016 presidential campaign. The hackers were successful in gaining access to thousands of confidential campaign emails.

port details how the Russians and WikiLeaks timed the release of the DNC emails to create conflict between the Clinton and Sanders camps during the party's convention. But experts on election security say the most important outcome of the Mueller investigation might be a greater awareness of how Russia could attack US political campaigns in 2020. As California secretary of state Alex Padilla declares, "For elections officials across the country, the Mueller investigation and indictments have heightened our need for additional resources to defend against cyber attacks."[8]

Taking the Threat Seriously

A major step for political campaigns in 2020 is to take the threat of Russian hacking seriously—and that means spending money for cyberdefenses. Campaigns generally are reluctant to divert scarce dollars from day-to-day operations into security. Yet experts warn that leaving computer files and email systems unprotected is an invitation to malicious cyber-criminals. Also, since campaigns operate on a short-term basis, they tend not to have well-developed protocols for cybersecurity among staffers. "The reason campaigns are so bad at cybersecurity is they are here one day and gone the next," says Aaron Trujillo, former chief of staff of the DCCC. "There needs to be a person who has to wake up every single day with part of their mission being how they are going to address threats and mitigate damage if there is a breach."[9]

> **"The reason campaigns are so bad at cybersecurity is they are here one day and gone the next."[9]**
>
> —Aaron Trujillo, former chief of staff of the DCCC

Plenty of tech companies are anxious to advise campaigns on cybersecurity. Many are willing to provide their services for free or at lower rates. Yet campaign officials are leery of violating campaign finance laws by accepting services at a reduced rate, which might be considered an illegal contribution. In May 2019 the Federal Election Commission (FEC) took action to relieve this concern. FEC chair Ellen Weintraub issued a ruling that allowed Defending Digital Campaigns, a nonprofit group, to offer free and low-cost cybersecurity services to political campaigns without running afoul of campaign finance laws. The group is a spinoff of Harvard's Defending Digital Democracy project. It was specifically created to help campaigns defend themselves against hacking attempts. Weintraub says the ruling was necessary to guard against foreign cyberattacks and that the federal government needs to do more to protect political parties and campaigns from foreign hackers.

Matt Rhoades, one of the board members for Defending Digital Campaigns, served as Mitt Romney's campaign manager in Romney's run for president in 2012. He knows how much cash-strapped campaigns will benefit from the ruling. "When you're first setting up and you're first raising those precious hard dollars," says Rhoades, "the last thing you want to do is to spend them on something to secure your networks."[10]

Sharing Information About Hacking Attacks

Another way political campaigns can thwart hackers is to share information about hacking attempts and about their cybersecurity systems in general. To support this idea, the US Department of Homeland Security (DHS) provides advice to campaigns on cybersecurity in its *Cybersecurity Services Catalog for Election Infrastructure*. This catalog lists cybersecurity services available to campaigns and state and local election offices. The DHS also maintains a network for sharing cyberthreat indicators in real time,

A Ruling That Boosts Cybersecurity for Campaigns

In July 2019 the FEC made a key decision that could help political campaigns avoid hacking attacks by Russia or other nations. The FEC ruled that campaigns can use discounted cybersecurity services as long as tech firms offer the same deals to nonpolitical customers. FEC lawyers had questioned whether use of such services was a violation of campaign finance laws. The laws seek to prevent corporations from providing candidates with reduced-rate products or services in exchange for political favors.

The FEC ruling focused on Area 1, a California-based cybersecurity company that specializes in detecting phishing schemes. Area 1 was started in 2013 by former National Security Agency hackers. The firm claims the ability to analyze billions of domains and web addresses every two weeks. Area 1 had asked the FEC whether it could offer its low-cost services to political candidates in the United States. The company noted that in 2018 the FEC allowed Microsoft to provide political candidates with account security for free. In that case, FEC officials decided that Microsoft risked damage to its reputation should its clients suffer hacking attacks like those in 2016. After initially hesitating, the FEC granted Area 1's request. Officials found that Area 1 charges the same fixed fee of $1,337 for its anti-phishing services to both campaigns and nonpolitical clients. As tech reporter Amrita Khalid observes, "Hopefully, this most recent FEC ruling will make it easier for campaigns and cybersecurity vendors to work together."

Amrita Khalid, "FEC Rules That Campaigns Can Get Discounts on Cybersecurity," *Engadget* (blog), July 11, 2019. www.engadget.com.

such as fake IP addresses or the email addresses associated with those who send phishing emails. When hackers do attempt to break into a campaign network, the DHS can provide remote assistance or send personnel to investigate. The DHS also maintains a hotline and troubleshooting website for cyberattacks.

The DHS takes care to ensure that campaigns that agree to share hacking information receive privacy protections. Nonetheless, campaign officials are mostly unwilling to share information about hacking attempts and cyberdefenses. They fear the information could somehow be leaked and used to breach their networks. In June 2019, when a reporter from the *Wall Street Journal* asked twenty-three Democratic presidential campaigns about cybersecurity, more than half declined to discuss their efforts. Joseph Lorenzo Hall, an election security expert at the nonprofit Center for Democracy & Technology, says campaigns are still lagging in cyberdefense and would benefit from sharing information about how they protect themselves from hackers. As Hall affirms, "Your best defense is the one you can tell your attackers about and still be secure."[11]

Using Multifactor Password Authentication

Campaigns can also beef up their cyberdefenses by improving their password security. A feature called multifactor authentication (MFA) provides a more secure method for staff members to access a campaign's computer network. Experts say this feature would almost certainly have foiled the successful Russian spear-phishing attack on Podesta's emails. In the email with the notorious typo, the tech person told Podesta to change his password and make sure that two-factor authentication was turned on.

Most campaigns today have adopted MFA, which is also employed by many banks and businesses. With MFA, when a user tries to access a network, he or she must present two or more independent credentials. This involves some combination of a user name and password, a secondary password or security token, and a biometric key, such as a fingerprint or retina scan. MFA sets up a defense with multiple layers to make it more difficult for unauthorized people to gain access to the network. Even if attackers manage to break through one barrier, they still must breach one or two more before they can break into the system. A typical MFA might require a staffer to key in a password, receive a random numerical code on a separate authorized device, and then key in the code for access. MFA helps solve the problem of maintaining a password database. Should sophisticated hackers capture a campaign's password database, even if it is encrypted, they can use it to eventually hack into the network.

MFA also helps guard against complacency among staff members. Requiring more than one authentication means that an easy-to-remember—and easy to hack—password like a person's name, birth date, child's name, or the word *password* is not relied on for security. Mueller's indictments noted that Russian hackers scoured email accounts for keywords like *password* or

Multifactor authentication (MFA) provides a more secure method to access a campaign's computer network. An MFA may require a user to receive a random numerical code on an authorized cell phone to then gain access to a network.

credit card in order to determine users' passwords for other accounts. MFA is not foolproof, but security experts say it is a strong defense against hacking. "There's not one single thing out there that can keep you perfectly safe," says Jamie Winterton, director of strategy at the Global Security Initiative at Arizona State University. "But there are a lot of different things out there that can keep you almost perfectly safe."[12] Some cybersecurity steps are simple but effective. For example, campaign staffers can help protect their systems by getting rid of old emails and text messages every thirty days. Campaigns should also update security patches for their software.

"There's not one single thing out there that can keep [your computer network] perfectly safe. But there are a lot of different things out there that can keep you almost perfectly safe."[12]

—Jamie Winterton, director of strategy at the Global Security Initiative at Arizona State University

Anti-hacking Support from Tech Companies

To foil the threat from foreign hackers, tech companies in the United States are offering targeted solutions. Cylance provides campaigns with antivirus software designed to detect and deter hacking attempts. Companies such as Cloudflare and Jigsaw protect campaign websites from attacks called distributed denial of service (DDoS). In a DDoS attack, a computer system is flooded with traffic from multiple sources in order to shut it down. Valimail has an email antifraud service that defends against so-called spoofing, in which hackers create a fake domain made to look like a campaign's website.

As part of its Defending Democracy Program, Microsoft now offers AccountGuard, a package of extra account security tools for political campaigns and think tanks. The tools include cybersecurity training for campaign staffers to help them identify and avoid account breaches. Microsoft's threat intelligence division also provides notifications when a hacking attempt by a foreign government is detected. AccountGuard currently protects more than thirty-six thousand email accounts in twenty-six countries. Already the program has issued hundreds of threat notifications about hackers.

The Mueller Report's detailed account of Russian hacking in the 2016 presidential election has campaigns scrambling to protect themselves in 2020. Cybersecurity experts warn that Russia and other nations are likely to launch similar attacks on campaigns, think tanks, and political advisors. To defend against hackers, experts say, campaigns should shore up their password protections, be alert to sophisticated spear-phishing ploys, and be prepared to share information about hacking attempts. And they should expect attacks through email. "Bad actors are trying to disrupt our elections and sow chaos in our democracy," says Valimail chief executive officer (CEO) Alexander Garcia-Tobar. "They are targeting email because it is one of the weakest points in digital communications."[13]

Spreading Fake News on Social Media

In August 2019 the FEC sent out invitations to a meeting that would address a hot topic related to the 2020 presidential election: fake news. According to the FEC, the attempt to fool voters with fraudulent stories about candidates and current events is a prime method of election interference. Ellen Weintraub, chair of the FEC, was calling on social media giants Facebook, Google, and Twitter to attend the daylong meeting, along with journalists, academics, and representatives from both major political parties. The purpose of the meeting was to identify ways to reduce bogus news stories and propaganda in the 2020 campaign.

Political analysts warn that fake news and false information can spread like wildfire on social media during the heat of a campaign. FEC officials fear that the purveyors of fake news may include not only foreign sources like Russia but also domestic groups bent on gaining a political advantage. FEC officials are seeking ways to curb deceptive news stories and political ads without stepping on free speech protections. "Under the First Amendment, we don't ban false statements in advertising and social media," says one FEC official, "but there's a difference between the right to speak and the right to be disseminated [spread]"[14] online.

Promoting Fake News

The term *fake news* has quickly become an essential part of America's political vocabulary. The hashtag #FakeNews is appended to tweets in order to question their truthfulness. President Trump uses the term frequently to refer to the media in general or to news stories about him or his administration that he disagrees with. An example is his tweet of August 5, 2018: "The Fake News hates me saying that they are the Enemy of the People only because they know it's TRUE. I am providing a great service by explaining this to the American People."[15]

Trump has often promulgated fake news himself. For example, FEC chair Weintraub has stated that there is no evidence for Trump's contention that he lost the popular vote in 2016 because of election fraud. Trump's critics note that his extensive use of Twitter enables him to spread false information and recycle fake news from other sources. When accused sex offender Jeffrey Epstein was found dead in his New York jail cell on August 10, 2019, from an apparent suicide, Trump retweeted conspiracy theories claiming that Epstein was actually murdered. The medical examiner in New York City later concluded that Epstein's death was indeed a suicide. Social media gives the president a quick and easy way to share his ideas with his online followers. News outlets are kept busy fact-checking Trump's claims and trying to debunk them. In addition, analysts say, it is more difficult for the federal government to combat fake news related to elections when the president himself contributes to the confusion.

Nonetheless, political experts worry most about the creation of fake news by hostile foreign governments, such as Russia. They fear an onslaught of false news stories and bogus websites in an attempt to interfere with the 2020 election. Some analysts believe Russian-sponsored fake news may have helped derail Hillary Clinton's 2016 campaign. In a December 2016 speech, Clinton mentioned "the epidemic of malicious fake news and false propaganda that [has] flooded social media over the past year." She went on to observe, "It's now clear that so-called fake news can have real-world consequences. This isn't about politics or partisanship. Lives are at risk . . . lives of ordinary people just trying to go about their days, to do their jobs, contribute to their communities."[16]

Clinton might have been referring to one of the most outlandish examples of fake news: the so-called Pizzagate episode. Beginning in early November 2016, a story online claimed that John Podesta's stolen emails contained coded references to a sex slave ring operating in the basement of a pizza restaurant in downtown Washington, DC. Right-wing foes of Clinton helped the tale go viral on social media. One man took the story so seriously that he stormed the restaurant with a loaded rifle and fired three shots inside. He was arrested before anyone was hurt.

"It's now clear that so-called fake news can have real-world consequences. This isn't about politics or partisanship."[16]

—Hillary Clinton, 2016 Democratic presidential candidate

President Donald Trump tweets #FakeNews frequently for news stories he does not like and to protest what he claims are made-up stories. He has been accused of promoting fake news himself through Twitter.

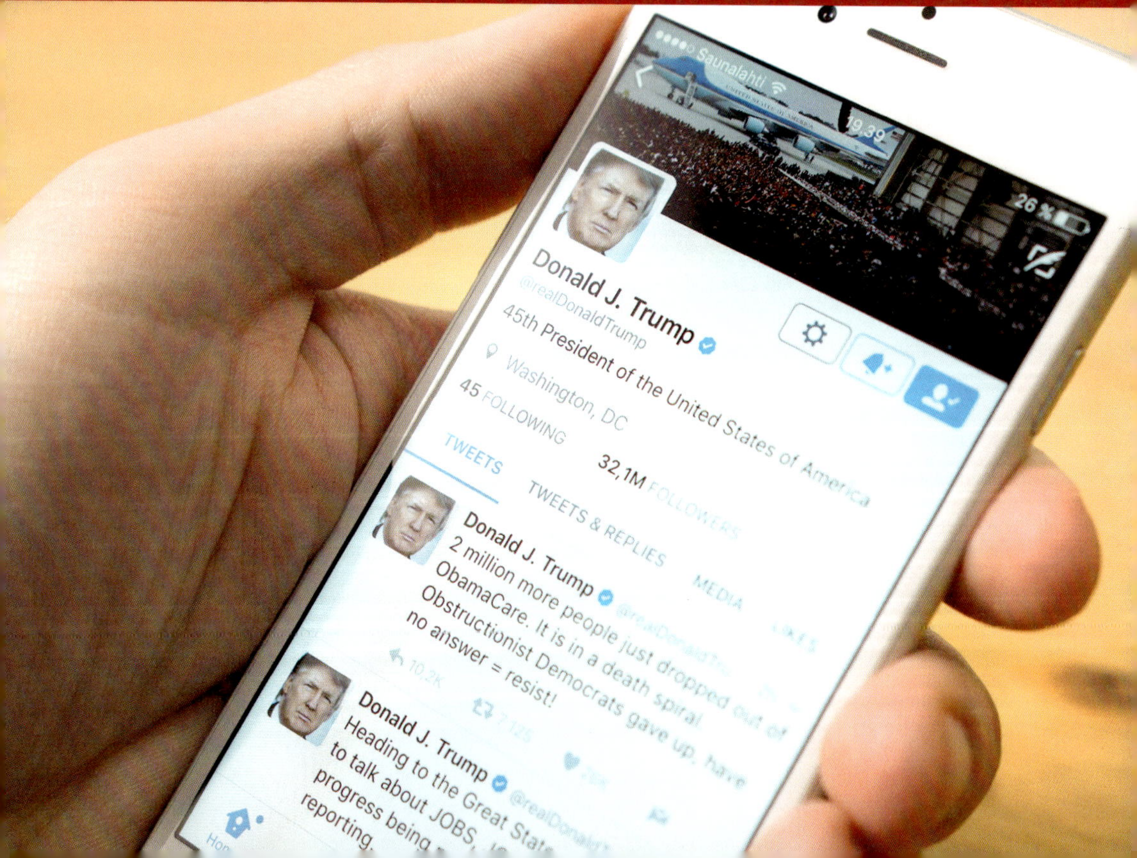

Troll Farms and Disinformation

Russia's scheme to disrupt America's presidential election with fake news began as early as 2014. According to the Mueller Report, three Russian companies, including the Kremlin-linked Internet Research Agency (IRA), set up "troll farms" to spread false information on social media. These were networks of fake accounts aimed at "trolling"; that is, posting inflammatory statements intended to stir up animosity online. This form of deception, called disinformation, hearkens back to the Soviet Union's propaganda efforts in the Cold War. Disinformation is designed to sow confusion and distrust among citizens, leading them to question the bedrock beliefs of their own society. Social media, with its far-flung and ever-shifting networks of users, is proving to be the perfect vehicle for the rapid spread of disinformation.

The IRA set up its first accounts on Facebook, YouTube, and Twitter and later added accounts on Tumblr and Instagram. "IRA employees operated social media accounts and group pages designed to attract U.S. audiences," says the Mueller Report. "These groups and accounts, which addressed divisive U.S. political and social issues, falsely claimed to be controlled by U.S. activists."[17] By 2016, with interest in the upcoming election at a fever pitch, the IRA and other Russian online networks were taking full advantage of Americans' appetite for political news and partisan attacks. Articles might claim that a candidate was guilty of tax evasion, gravely ill, or accused of murder. The Mueller Report estimates that more than 126 million Americans on Facebook accessed fake accounts, groups, and advertisements created by the IRA. Russian-created posts on Instagram reached another 26 million.

Russian trolls concentrated on hot-button issues certain to attract interest, such as gun control, immigration, and the Black Lives Matter movement. A Russian-led Facebook group with the name Secured Borders—a major Trump campaign theme—garnered more than 130,000 followers, while another one called Being Patriotic had over 200,000. Media outlets from NBC News to the *New York Times* unknowingly reported on tweets from IRA-created Twitter accounts as if they had come from genuine political source. In cities like Miami and Philadelphia, Russian trolls were able to organize rallies that attracted hundreds of people. Those in attendance had no idea that the Russians were behind them.

According to Mueller, the focus of the Russian trolling effort was anti-Clinton and pro-Trump. One ad depicted a red-faced Hillary Clinton with Satan horns, and another placed her photo in a police lineup. Russian-backed Twitter communities pushed the hashtags #HillaryClintonForPrison2016 and #nohillary2016. The IRA also made sure that stories about the DNC's stolen emails—courtesy of Russian hackers—were shared by bogus Facebook groups and Twitter feeds. By contrast, ads about Trump tended to have a positive spin. The Mueller Report found that the Trump campaign actually promoted many Facebook posts and tweets concocted by the IRA without knowing their source.

Most worrisome to many political analysts is how much coverage the Russian trolls achieved despite small expenditures. Facebook estimates that the IRA spent about $46,000 on fake sites and advertisements on its platform—this in a presidential election that saw the two major campaigns spend a combined $81 million on Facebook ads. The Russians used sensationalism to get more bang for their buck. As tech reporter Josh Constine observes, "By focusing on hot-button issues and playing into people's biases, the IRA's ads got widely re-shared for free by viewers."[18]

Turning Up the Heat on Social Media

Experts have little doubt that Russian trolls will be pushing fake news and propaganda once more in the 2020 election. They urge voters to be aware of how social media sites can be manipulated for political ends. With Americans deeply divided over candidates and issues, the 2020 campaign is ripe for manipulation by outside forces. And Russian troll farms like the IRA are doubtless developing new methods to create fake news and bogus websites. They seek to influence public opinion with their

Following Russia's Lead on Fake News

With the United States occupying such a dominant position in world affairs, other nations have a large stake in who wins the presidential election in 2020. China is seeking more accommodating trade policies from the United States. Iran no doubt desires an end to the biting sanctions imposed on its economy by the Trump administration. Political analysts say these nations, along with Russia, will likely resort to their own campaigns of fake news and disinformation in an effort to influence the US election.

China's government has shown recently how it can use social media and disinformation to manipulate public opinion. State-sponsored media in China portrayed peaceful prodemocracy protests in Hong Kong as violently out of control. A widely shared item on Weibo, China's version of Twitter, showed a tourist from Shanghai allegedly being roughed up at a Hong Kong rally. Twitter banned Chinese-sponsored media ads on its platform after observers noticed fifty ads presenting the Hong Kong protests as violent and anti-Chinese. Twitter also announced it had removed more than nine hundred accounts that it said were obvious attempts to stir up political feelings against the Hong Kong protesters. Informed about the propaganda outlets on Twitter, Facebook removed similar accounts and pages from its own platform. Political analysts expect China and other nations to adopt Russia's methods as the 2020 election approaches. According to Doug Bandow, a senior fellow at the Cato Institute, "I would expect that it will grow as other countries and movements seek to follow the example they see elsewhere."

Quoted in James Varney, "Russia's Playbook: China, Iran Push 'Fake News' to Spark Social Discord," *Washington Times* (Washington, DC), May 27, 2019. www.washingtontimes.com.

deceptive articles and posts. In 2016 Russian trolls even tried to affect voters' behavior. They attempted to fool readers into texting their votes or urged people to vote for third-party candidates like Jill Stein. Some posts argued that voting for president was a waste of time and encouraged voters to stay home on Election Day. Analysts expect the IRA to double down on such messages in 2020.

After the 2016 election, social media companies like Facebook felt the heat about all the fake news on their sites. Critics blasted their lack of control over what they published. Furious progressives blamed Facebook for helping Trump win the White

House. In April 2018 Facebook founder Mark Zuckerberg was summoned before a joint Senate committee to explain his company's failures regarding fake news. In his testimony, Zuckerberg shouldered the blame:

> It's clear now that we didn't do enough to prevent these tools from being used for harm as well. That goes for fake news, foreign interference in elections, and hate speech, as well as developers and data privacy. We didn't take a broad enough view of our responsibility, and that was a big mistake. It was my mistake, and I'm sorry. I started Facebook, I run it, and I'm responsible for what happens here.[19]

Congress has demanded that social media companies take steps to eliminate fake news from their platforms. Facebook tried using outside fact-checking groups to verify whether stories were

Facebook founder Mark Zuckerberg testifies in 2018 before a joint Senate committee to explain Facebook's failures regarding fake news. Zuckerberg admitted that the company did not do enough to combat the spread of false or misleading information.

genuine. However, this process proved to be awkward and unreliable. Cyber experts say a better plan is to increase communication between social media platforms, such as Instagram, Twitter, and YouTube, that have had problems with false information. This will help social media companies share concerns about specific users or ad buyers. Facebook and Instagram have also begun a policy in which advertisers running ads on politics or social issues must post their contact information to demonstrate they are legitimate. In 2016 and 2018 some political ads had "paid for by" disclaimers listing groups that did not exist. Under the new rules, political advertisers must provide a US mailing address and identification document, a phone number, business email, and website link.

Detecting Fake News with Artificial Intelligence

To combat the Russian trolls, Facebook and other social media companies have turned to a technological fix: artificial intelligence, or AI. They are working on AI programs that can identify false or deceptive material through machine learning. Generally, these are fairly simple programs that employ analytics to flag language that is strongly partisan—with the possible drawback of censoring protected political speech. But social media may soon have a more effective weapon to fend off fake news.

Researchers at the Massachusetts Institute of Technology (MIT) are using AI to create automated fake news detectors that are more sophisticated. These networks can analyze scores of news articles, both genuine and fake, in order to learn how language cues differ between them. The networks create a list of words and phrases that help them predict when an article is not real news. The AI system identifies sets of words that appear much more frequently in fake news articles. Often these are words that exaggerate or offer over-the-top praise or blame, as opposed to the more measured language of real news sources.

Once the networks "learn" how to detect the language of false articles, they can apply the test for news throughout the Internet.

As the networks improve, they can even examine topics they have not seen in training. For now, while not foolproof, the AI networks show great promise for addressing the fake news epidemic. "Fake news is a threat for democracy," says Xavier Boix, a coauthor of the MIT study. "It would be powerful to have tools for users or companies that could provide an assessment of whether news is fake or not."[20]

> "Fake news is a threat for democracy. It would be powerful to have tools for users or companies that could provide an assessment of whether news is fake or not."[20]
>
> —Xavier Boix, coauthor of a study on detecting fake news with AI

Dangers of Deepfake Technology

While AI offers promise as a tool for recognizing fake news, it has also been deployed by those who wish to create fake news. Using AI programs, trolls can alter videos and photographs in ways that are difficult for ordinary people to detect. This technique, called deepfake technology, threatens to cast doubt on the whole idea of "seeing is believing." In a digital culture so attuned to gathering information visually on screens and phones, deepfake technology could become the ultimate in fake news.

For example, in May 2019 a deepfake video of Speaker of the House Nancy Pelosi made the rounds on the Internet, garnering 2.5 million views on Facebook. In the doctored video, Pelosi's speech is slurred and she appears to be drunk. To create the clip, someone simply slowed the frame speed to 75 percent. Nonetheless, to someone unfamiliar with deepfake technology, the video looks real. This low-tech version of a deepfake shows how convincing it can be. Moreover, much more sophisticated deepfake techniques could be used to make a person appear to say something he or she never said.

Hany Farid, a professor of computer science at the University of California, Berkeley, believes that this kind of deepfake ploy could cause genuine confusion and panic. "What if somebody creates a video of President Trump saying, 'I've launched nuclear weapons against Iran, or North Korea, or Russia'?" asks Farid. "We don't have hours or days to figure out if it's real or not."[21] In the heat of an election, a candidate could be trolled with a fake video showing him or her making a radical policy shift or a racist remark. Audio deepfakes are potentially disastrous. In September 2019 an AI-assisted phone voice scam fooled the CEO of an energy firm in the United Kingdom into transferring nearly a quarter million dollars to the scammer's account. Moreover, this deepfake technology is available to anyone—including Russian outfits like the IRA. The US government's Worldwide Threat Assessment has warned that foreign adversaries are likely to use deepfakes to disrupt the 2020 election.

In May 2019 a deepfake video of Speaker of the House Nancy Pelosi (pictured) garnered 2.5 million views on Facebook. In the doctored video, Pelosi's speech is slurred and she appears to be intoxicated.

Election Mischief, Both Foreign and Domestic

Analysts predict that Russia will not be the only source of fake news and deepfake manipulation in 2020. A recent report from New York University's Stern Center for Business and Human Rights warns that Iran and China are also likely to generate disinformation to disrupt the election. Experts at the Stern Center note that Iran's anger over the Trump administration's sanctions increase the likelihood of fake news and disinformation from Iranian trolls. Iranian troll farms have already launched major Twitter campaigns about Brexit, the controversial withdrawal of Britain from the European Union, and other European political issues.

Trolling the African American Community

A major target of Russian trolls like the IRA has been the African American community. Of the dozen web domains registered to the IRA in 2016, most aimed to reach black Americans. Domain names drew on themes of the Black Lives Matter movement, with names like DoNotShoot.us and Blacktivist.info. Almost half of the most popular Facebook pages promoted by the IRA addressed black readers. Facebook ads targeted blacks who had shown interest in topics of African American history, such as the Black Panther Party and Malcolm X. On Instagram, an IRA-created account named @blackstagram attracted more than 300,000 followers and garnered 28 million responses. Of 1,100 YouTube videos linked to the IRA, 1,063 dealt with scenes of police brutality and Black Lives Matter issues. YouTube channels were labeled Don't Shoot and BlackToLive.

Political analysts note that the IRA's efforts echo those of the former Soviet Union's KGB (spy agency) during the Cold War. Like the KGB, Russian trolls today seek to highlight racial tensions in the United States and stir up resentment among black Americans. In 2016 these messages sought to depress the black vote—and Hillary Clinton's prospects—by sowing distrust in the American system. Experts expect similar trolling campaigns in 2020. "Very real racial tensions and feelings of alienation exist in America," says Renee DiResta, coauthor of a major report on Russian trolling commissioned by the US Senate. "The I.R.A. didn't create them. It exploits them."

Quoted in Scott Shane and Sheera Frenkel, "Russian 2016 Influence Operation Targeted African-Americans on Social Media," *New York Times*, December 17, 2019. www.nytimes.com.

Trump's trade war with China could spur that country to promote fake news and political attacks as well.

> "If an information consumer does not know what to believe, [if] they can't tell fact from fiction, then they will either believe everything or they will believe nothing at all."[23]
>
> —Clint Watts of the Foreign Policy Research Institute

The report also contends that domestic purveyors of fake news outnumber foreign sources. "While foreign election interference has dominated discussion of contemporary disinformation, most purposely false content in the US is generated by domestic sources," say the authors. "That's the consensus of social media executives, cybersecurity sleuths, and academic researchers."[22] The report warns that trolls in the United States may try to suppress the vote by spreading bogus information. The authors note that in the 2018 midterm elections, some trolls repeatedly posted the incorrect day to vote.

Political analysts expect an onslaught of fake news and disinformation in the lead-up to the 2020 presidential election. Russian troll farms like the IRA seem likely to create fake news and disinformation on social media sites in an attempt to disrupt the election. Other foreign and domestic trolls are also liable to purvey false information. In response, federal government agencies and social media companies are gearing up to identify and eliminate fake news stories and deceptive posts. As Clint Watts of the Foreign Policy Research Institute told a congressional committee in June 2019, "If an information consumer does not know what to believe, [if] they can't tell fact from fiction, then they will either believe everything or they will believe nothing at all. If they believe nothing at all, that leads to long-term apathy, and that is destructive for the United States."[23]

Tampering with Voter Databases

One sentence in the Mueller Report drew special interest from election officials in Florida. It is included in a section on Russia's attempts to break into the computer systems of state election boards, secretaries of state, and employees at state agencies. The report notes that in 2016 Russian hackers sent more than 120 spear-phishing emails to election offices in Florida counties. Florida officials had been told by the DHS that the hacking attempts had failed. However, the Mueller Report casts doubt on that conclusion. As it notes, "The F.B.I. believes that this operation enabled the G.R.U. [Russian equivalent of the CIA] to gain access to the network of at least one Florida county government."[24] Russian hackers seemed to have broken through to voter rolls, registration details, and other election-related material in Florida. The Mueller Report does not say the breach resulted in any change in voting results, but the suspicion left some Florida officials angrily demanding that federal authorities share their findings. "They won't tell us which county it was. Are you kidding me?" said Florida governor Ron DeSantis. "Why would you have not said something immediately?"[25]

Hacking Election Board Computers

State officials like DeSantis were frustrated to learn that Russian hackers—military officers working for Russia's GRU—had successfully breached election board computers. They feared that Florida might have suffered the same fate as Illinois had in June

Voters wait in line at a polling center. Hackers who access voter data can spread misinformation such as incorrect polling locations and dates.

2016 when hackers broke into the Illinois voter registration database and, before the hack was discovered, were able to download personal details of about five hundred thousand voters. Officials like DeSantis know that the security of voter rolls and registration information is essential to maintaining public trust in the election process. That is why he demanded more federal cooperation to identify the problem and to foil future hacking attempts.

Election boards maintain voter databases, or voter rolls, on computer networks. The databases are continually updated to ensure they are accurate. Voter registration data, including each voter's name and party affiliation among other facts, are generally made available to political campaigns, since they need to know who their voters are. Many states also provide voter lists to the public upon request. However, hackers have a more sinister purpose for seeking this data. If hackers are able to penetrate state election board computer systems, they can use voter data to spread misinformation to voters of a certain party. They can even deceive them about the date of the election or the location of polling places. Should hackers delete voters from the rolls, legitimate votes could be called into question. In a close election, the hacked rolls of even one county could provide the hackers' preferred candidate or party a margin of victory.

The hacking attack in Florida was a typical spear-phishing ploy, detected only the day before the 2016 election. Lisa Lewis, Florida's supervisor of elections, noticed a week-old email that had been sent to her computer and three others in her office. The email supposedly was from VR Systems, a vendor of electronic equipment for voter databases that operates in every county in the state. Lewis thought the email looked suspicious, especially since it was from a Gmail account, which VR Systems had never used before. Sure enough, Lewis soon found another email from VR's usual address alerting customers to a possible hacking attempt and warning them not to click on the attached link. The phony email carried a Trojan horse virus capable of infecting computers with one click. More than 120 election board email accounts throughout Florida had received the Russians' spear-phishing email. And apparently, at least one employee had clicked on the link and activated the virus.

Playing Down the Threat

In April 2019 US senator from Florida Marco Rubio confirmed the Mueller Report's suspicions about the Florida hack. According to Rubio, Russian hackers had not only breached Florida's voter rolls but were also in a position to alter voter roll data. When federal investigators detected the hack, they issued a blanket warning about hacking attempts on state election boards. However, they refrained from notifying election officials about the hacks so as not to reveal intelligence sources. It was the FBI's secretiveness that left DeSantis so exasperated.

After its agents briefed DeSantis, the FBI issued a statement declaring it had not found any hacking activity that affected vote counts or disrupted election processes in the previous two national elections. Nonetheless, Rubio sees trouble ahead in 2020 if the hacking threat is not addressed. As he told the *New York Times*, "My biggest concern is that on Election Day you go vote and have mass confusion because voter registration information has been deleted from the systems."[26]

"My biggest concern is that on Election Day you go vote and have mass confusion because voter registration information has been deleted from the systems."[26]

—US senator Marco Rubio

Just three months after Rubio's warning, the Senate Intelligence Committee revealed that the Russian hacking effort was far more widespread than previously thought. The committee issued a report, heavily redacted—that is, with many lines blacked out for security purposes—saying that the Russians had targeted election computer systems in all fifty states. The report describes an intelligence failure that spiraled

In 2019 US senator from Florida Marco Rubio (shown) confirmed the Mueller Report's suspicions about a hack of the Florida voter rolls. According to Rubio, Russian hackers breached voter rolls and gained access to voting data.

down from Washington, DC, to state election officials to election board employees. According to the report, federal officials had underestimated the Russians' hacking capabilities, their warnings to the states were not forceful enough, and state officials either downplayed the threat or disregarded agents' attempts to help.

Some analysts worry that the threat still is not taken seriously enough. Computer experts say Russian hackers might have planted malware—malicious software—in the election board computers, like little time bombs that could destroy voter information at some later time. At any rate, political writer Charles P. Pierce finds it hard

Selling Voter Data on the Dark Web

As the 2020 election approaches, hackers are peddling downloaded voter records in the hidden corners of the Internet. According to cybersecurity firms Anomali Labs and Intel 471, the voter records downloaded from nineteen states number more than 35 million. They are being offered for sale in hacker forums on the so-called dark web. This part of the Internet does not appear on search engine indexes and requires special authorization or passwords for access. Since activity on the dark web is virtually untraceable, it plays host to many criminal transactions, including sales of drugs, firearms, and personal information. Researchers Daniel Moore and Thomas Rid of King's College London have found that 57 percent of dark web sites trade in illicit material.

The voter records being offered for sale include personal details such as full name, phone numbers, addresses, and voting histories. "I want to make clear that the information posted is publicly available information," says Dan Barahona, chief marketing officer at Anomali. "We are not suggesting any states have been hacked." Nonetheless, the very fact that the voter records are being marketed on the dark web indicates some shady objective. For example, cybercriminals could combine the voter data with stolen Social Security numbers to perpetrate identify theft. The records could also be used to tamper with election results. According to Barahona, "Someone attempting to impact elections could use this information to register on behalf of other voters, request mail-in ballots and vote early as those voters, for example."

Quoted in Brooke Crothers, "35 Million Voter Records Up for Sale on the Dark Web," *New York Post*, October 19, 2019. www.nypost.com.

to believe the FBI's story that the hacks on state election board computer systems basically did no damage:

> Remember when we were told that it was only a couple of precincts, then a couple of cities, then a couple of states? Remember when it was just data? Now, as far as we can read between the blacked-out lines, we are being asked to believe that the [Russians] could have deleted "voter data," that they "were in a position" to jack around with it, but, having achieved this monumental intelligence triumph, *they didn't do anything with it?* Does that dog even look like it's hunting any more?[27]

Fifty Different Security Systems

Federal agencies play only a limited role in protecting voter databases from malicious hackers. That is because voting procedures in the United States are left to the states, and each state has its own security system for elections and voter databases. In general, voter lists are public records available to anyone. Under the 2002 Help America Vote Act, states are required to create centralized voter databases and make the data available upon request.

States, however, can decide how much information to disclose from their voter databases and how that information can be used. For example, Florida has no limits on how voter data can be used. New York and California restrict the usage of voter data to only commercial purposes, such as advertising or marketing products to voters. Voter rolls in every state contain at least name, address, and party affiliation for

"We are being asked to believe that the [Russians] could have deleted 'voter data,' that they 'were in a position' to jack around with it, but, having achieved this monumental intelligence triumph, *they didn't do anything with it?*"[27]

—Political writer Charles P. Pierce

each voter. They also record whether a voter participated in each election, although not the candidates he or she voted for. Some states, such as Florida and Texas, include more personal data about voters, such as email address, date of birth, and race. This information can be valuable for hackers planning a disinformation attack to influence voters during a campaign.

Requests for voter data are generally handled at the county level. This means that cybersecurity protections vary widely, with some counties much more vulnerable to hacking than others. As information technology (IT) professional Monica Pal observes,

> The problem is county registrars, individual campaigns and specialty vendors are not cybersecurity-savvy. Online data requests are often verified based on phone calls or emails that can be spoofed, and these small organizations are soft targets for even unsophisticated cybercriminals.[28]

Pal says her company, GCN, found that more than 60 million voter records were hacked in 2017 and more than 70 million in 2018. These records, stolen from nineteen states, have circulated online, leaving voters open to scams, influence campaigns, and identify theft.

Democrats in Congress say the solution is to set mandatory national standards for cybersecurity, instead of leaving it up to states and localities. They believe federal agencies should oversee state efforts to prevent hacking of voter databases. "We would not ask a local sheriff to go to war against the missiles, planes and tanks of the Russian Army," says Senator Ron Wyden, a Democrat from Oregon. "We shouldn't ask a county election IT employee to fight a war against the

"We shouldn't ask a county election IT employee to fight a war against the full capabilities and vast resources of Russia's cyber army. That approach failed in 2016 and it will fail again."[29]

—Senator Ron Wyden, a Democrat from Oregon

An Opening to Voter Rolls and Poll Books

Voters have been assured that the actual voting process in the United States is safe from hackers. Yet investigators have found that a Florida election software company may have accidentally left a pathway open for potential hackers on the day before the 2016 presidential election. VR Systems, a software firm with customers in eight states, used so-called remote-access software to connect with a central election office computer in Durham, North Carolina. The purpose was to troubleshoot possible glitches with VR's voter list management tool. The software sends voter lists to electronic poll books, which are used by poll workers to check in voters and verify that they are eligible to vote. The remote connection left Durham's computer vulnerable to hackers for several hours.

Election security experts take a dim view of remote-access connections like the one VR Systems used in this case. Such connections can enable hackers to gain access to a whole network. The Durham computer was linked to North Carolina's Board of Elections and its database of voter registration records. Hackers could have changed these records to keep people from voting in key precincts. Apparently, it was not uncommon for VR Systems to perform this kind of remote troubleshooting to save their employees from making a service call in person. According to Matt Blaze, a professor at Georgetown Law and longtime expert on election security, "If poll books are compromised, this can selectively disenfranchise voters, create long lines at polling places, and cast doubt on the legitimacy of election results."

Quoted in Kim Zetter, "Software Vendor May Have Opened a Gap for Hackers in 2016 Swing State," *Politico*, June 5, 2019. www.politico.com.

full capabilities and vast resources of Russia's cyber army. That approach failed in 2016 and it will fail again."[29] In September 2019, Republican Senate majority leader Mitch McConnell relented slightly and agreed to $250 million in spending on election security.

Back to Basics of Cybersecurity

Experts say states seem to be improving their cybersecurity for voter databases by going back to the basics. This means installing new security software on networks or updating the current version to eliminate vulnerable areas. More than $800 million was spent nationwide on shoring up elections systems with hardware and software updates. Thousands of county election workers received training on the updates as well. Another basic fix is for election board employees to use stronger passwords and two-factor authentication when accessing voter databases. These measures must include all the personal devices that employees use to gain access to voter information. This could include laptops, phones, and tablets.

States also have made strides in limiting employee access to voter databases and voter registration material. Some offices divide up access privileges so that lower-level employees can only link to the data necessary for them to do their jobs. If only a few authorized personnel have the ability to access sensitive material, the opportunities for hackers are greatly reduced.

"What states and local jurisdictions need to get right is keeping in mind this is not an end process, it's ongoing. . . . It's not one and done. You need to keep getting it right."[30]

—Thomas MacLellan, head of policy and government affairs at cybersecurity firm Symantec

Thomas MacLellan, head of policy and government affairs at cybersecurity firm Symantec, says the improvements are welcome but warns that election officials must constantly be on guard. "What states and local jurisdictions need to get right is keeping in mind this is not an end process, it's ongoing," says MacLellan. "It's no different than any security situation. It's not one and done. You need to keep getting it right. Use peer intelligence, use basic security hygiene. It has to be an ongoing initiative."[30]

Security experts also urge state and county election board officials to share information about voter database protection and breaches. They say it is important to sound the alarm if there is a security breach so other states can take precautions. However, some election officials remain leery of revealing too much, even to researchers and colleagues in other states. They worry that publicizing details of their security efforts will somehow lead to successful hacks. Eric Rosenbach, director of the Defending Digital Democracy project at Harvard, says it is a question of trust. "It's a real weakness," says Rosenbach, "because you need to get the facts out and engage with the public to develop trust in the system."[31]

Defending Against Ransomware Attacks

In shoring up their cyberdefenses, state and county election officials should remember that Russian hackers might try techniques that have worked against other government agencies and some businesses. Experts point to recent so-called ransomware attacks as examples of a possible disaster. Ransomware is a hacking tool that can lock down data, making it unavailable to users, or shut down a computer system altogether. It gets its name because hackers use it to demand a ransom payment before they will unfreeze the system. If payment is not received, hackers can use the malicious software to wipe out entire databases. Experts fear that ransomware could open a whole new front in the cyberwar on elections.

Like most computer hacks, ransomware is spread through phishing in email attachments. In the past few months, hackers have perpetrated ransomware attacks on municipal computer systems in New York, Florida, Maryland, and Texas. In April 2019 a ransomware attack locked down city service computers in Albany, New York. As a result, police lost access to emails and schedules, while applications for copies of birth, death, and marriage certificates were put on hold. In June city councils in Lake City and Rivera Beach, two Florida cities, agreed to pay hackers a combined sum of more than $1 million to get their computer systems back online following a ransomware attack. In August twenty-three government computer systems in Texas were frozen by a coordinated ransomware attack. Most of the systems were run by small local government offices. Technicians were able to restore the Texas computers without ransom being paid.

Analysts believe foreign hackers could employ ransomware attacks on voter registration databases simply to sow confusion and distrust in the election process. Such an attack could prevent voters from registering or keep poll workers from checking databases to confirm that voters are eligible. The DHS fears that voter databases across the country are vulnerable to ransomware. The breached systems in 2016 may have been a warm-up for more serious attacks in 2020. According to DHS spokesperson Scott McConnell, "A successful ransomware attack at a critical point before an election could limit access to information and has the potential to undermine public confidence in the election itself."[32]

States are using various methods to guard against a ransomware attack. In Wisconsin state employees must authenti-

In August 2019 twenty-three government computer systems in Texas were frozen by a coordinated ransomware attack. A sign on an affected computer in a public library notifies patrons that its computer system is not working.

cate themselves with a token called a FIDO key, which enables them to log in to computer systems securely. Election workers in Illinois can access voter registration data only from a closed fiber-optic network, instead of the regular Internet. And all state and county employees are urged to back up their systems frequently and constantly be on the lookout for signs of an attempted hack.

Cybersecurity experts warn that voter databases on state and county computer systems are especially susceptible to hackers. Evidence that election office computer systems in all fifty states were hacked by Russians in the 2016 election has only deepened their concern. Some suggest that cybersecurity for the databases should be set by national policy, but others believe states and localities should maintain their own systems. In the meantime, to prevent tampering with voter registration databases, election workers are advised by experts to concentrate on the most basic security measures: more sophisticated passwords, updates in security software, and a sharp eye for possible breaches in the system.

CHAPTER FOUR

Interfering with the Voting Process

Voting machine vendors assure the public that their devices are not susceptible to hacking. However, many computer-savvy individuals disagree. To demonstrate, hackers at a Las Vegas, Nevada, conference in August 2019 attempted to hack into the same types of voting machines that are currently in use across the nation. Expert hackers attending the Def Con Hacking Conference, a large annual event to promote cybersecurity, were invited to a Voting Village, where they could test their skills on actual voting machines and evaluate them for weaknesses.

The hackers made short work of the machines. In a video posted by CNN, it took a hacker only a few minutes to break into a Diebold voting machine and establish top-level access. No special tools were required. This means votes could be changed or deleted at will. Diebold, which has sold off its voting machine business, made the industry-standard voting machines that are still in use in eighteen states. A number of hackers showed off by tampering creatively with voting machines made by other companies. One machine was turned into a multimedia device, blaring rock music and displaying animations. An electronic poll book was reprogrammed to play *Doom*, a popular computer game. Oregon senator Ron Wyden, a guest speaker at the event, was shocked at the ease with which hackathon participants could hack into the machines. “Election officials across the country as we speak are buying election systems that will be out of date the moment they open the box," Wyden told those in attendance. "It's the election security equivalent of putting our military out there to go up against superpowers with a peashooter."[33]

Vulnerable Voting Machines and Websites

Hackers in the Voting Village discovered other vulnerabilities. Many of the machines had links to the Internet, which meant they could be hacked remotely. This demolished claims from voting machine companies that the devices never connect to the Internet and are immune from hacking. In fact, according to security experts, election systems in ten different states have been connected to the Internet at some point in the past year.

Websites designed to post election results proved to be even less secure. In another area of the conference, forty young hackers from ages six to seventeen tried their hands at breaking into closely modeled versions of the election sites. Most succeeded in changing vote totals. One hacker changed a candidate's name to Bob Da Builder. As an organizer of the event told CNN, "Unfortunately, it's so easy to hack the websites that report elections results"[34] that they did not bother giving this challenge to the adult hackers.

"Election officials across the country as we speak are buying election systems that will be out of date the moment they open the box. It's the election security equivalent of putting our military out there to go up against superpowers with a peashooter."[33]

—Ron Wyden, US senator from Oregon

Despite findings about Russian hacking in 2016, federal authorities insist that the voting process itself was not affected. As a July 2019 Senate Intelligence Committee report declares, "The committee has seen no evidence that any votes were changed or that any voting machines were manipulated."[35] But demonstrations like the ones at Def Con show that electronic voting machines are far from secure. A November 2018 survey from

Hackers at the Def Con Hacking Conference in Las Vegas, Nevada, pull apart computers used in voting machines during a contest to uncover potential security bugs in the systems.

California-based cybersecurity firm OpenVPN shows that a majority of voters are concerned. The survey found that 60 percent of Americans believe the US voting system is not secure. Sixty-three percent feel the United States has not done enough to shore up the voting system for future elections. If, as the NSA believes, Russians or other hackers are likely to attack US voting systems in 2020, more protections are still necessary to secure the voting process. Experts say the most pressing needs are providing paper backups for recording votes and replacing out-of-date voting equipment.

Creating a Paper Record for Votes

Security experts and political analysts have long noted the importance of paper backup records for voting. Having a physical record of votes on paper helps election officials perform a thorough audit of the vote. A voting audit is a careful review carried out after the polls close to determine that votes have been counted accurately. Such audits can be crucial to determining the outcome in a close election. Increasing numbers of politicians in both parties have called for voting machines in all states to have paper backups to facilitate the auditing process.

In June 2019 one of the largest manufacturers of voting machines in the United States joined this chorus in favor of paper records for voting machines. Tom Burt, CEO of Election Systems & Software (and unrelated to the Microsoft vice president), explained his company's decision on the political website Roll Call:

> Our company, Election Systems & Software, the nation's leading elections equipment provider, recently decided it will no longer sell paperless voting machines as the primary voting device in a jurisdiction. That's because it is difficult to perform a meaningful audit without a paper record of each voter's selections. Mandating the use of a physical paper record sets the stage for all jurisdictions to perform statistically valid postelection audits.[36]

Ironically, electronic voting machines were widely adopted because of perceived problems with paper ballots. In the 2000 presidential election, controversy raged after certain Florida counties had trouble counting votes recorded on punch cards. Many of the cards had punch marks for more than one candidate or were not punched sufficiently to make the voter's preference obvious. When vote counters in Florida were found to be using different standards for what a legal vote was, the US Supreme Court halted the recount, leaving George W. Bush the winner of the election.

"Mandating the use of a physical paper record [for voting machines] sets the stage for all jurisdictions to perform statistically valid postelection audits."[36]

—Tom Burt, CEO of Election Systems & Software

The controversy led to passage of the 2002 Help America Vote Act (HAVA), which gave states $3.9 billion to run federal elections. It also outlawed punch-card machines in favor of new electronic equipment. The new machines that states purchased were either optical-scan or direct-recording electronic machines. With optical-scan machines, voters fill out paper ballots and feed them into a scanner to record their votes. The paper ballots at least offer the opportunity to compare them with the digital tally, although this is rarely done. However, with direct-recording machines, voters use touch screens to make their choices on digital ballots, with no paper backups. Of the hundreds of thousands

An Unhackable Voting Machine?

One of the voting machines that hackers encountered at the 2019 Def Con conference in Las Vegas, Nevada, came from an unexpected source: the US government. The device, the product of a $10 million project, is a prototype designed to be completely secure. It was created through the Defense Advanced Research Projects Agency (DARPA), which serves as a workshop for technologies beyond the cutting edge. Scientists at the Oregon-based firm Galois designed everything about the new voting system. It even has specially created computer chips, instead of ones from chip makers like Intel or AMD. The idea is to develop a voting platform built from the ground up on secure hardware. DARPA believes the voting machine prototype could become the standard for secure devices for government and businesses.

Unlike the finished products at Def Con, the DARPA device is not ready to face hackers for the ultimate test. But hackers at the conference were impressed by what they saw. Voting on the device is done by touch screen, with the vote then confirmed and printed out. A voter's selections appear on the printout along with a special bar code. The printout sheet is fed into a ballot box to record the vote. DARPA hopes to have the finished version ready for next year's Def Con. "The goal of the program is to develop these tools to provide security against hardware vulnerabilities," says Linton Salmon, the project's manager at DARPA. "Our goal is to protect against remote attacks."

Quoted in Lily Hay Newman, "Hackers Take on Darpa's $10 Million Voting Machine," *Wired*, August 9, 2019. www.wired.com.

of voting machines set to be used in the 2020 election, it is estimated that about 12 percent will not create paper records for a manual recount. Five states currently produce no audit-ready records of votes on paper.

Risk from Aging Voting Machines

Even with federal money available for new equipment, many county election boards continue to rely on out-of-date voting machines. According to the Brennan Center for Justice, a nonpartisan law and policy institute, forty states are using voting machines that are least a decade old. Security experts warn that antiquated machines are more likely to malfunction. In the 2018 midterm elections, aged and malfunctioning voting machines forced voters in some states to wait in long lines at polling places. Some frustrated voters left without casting a ballot. Older machines lack features necessary to protect the integrity of the vote. The National Academy of Sciences suggests that if machines cannot create a printout of a voter's ballot selections for the voter to check, they should be replaced at once. Old voting machines also are more vulnerable to on-site tampering. As the Def Con hackers demonstrated, even industry-standard machines with the latest security protections are far from tamperproof. J. Alex Halderman, a computer scientist and election security expert at the University of Michigan, says he and his team have managed to hack into both touch screen and optical-scan voting machines in an experimental setting. According to Halderman, they were able to change votes—which, in an actual election, could potentially alter election outcomes—by introducing a virus that spread from machine to machine.

Congress has provided HAVA funding to address the issue of outdated voting machines. According to the US Election Assistance Commission, states are using $136 million of the HAVA funds to bolster cybersecurity for elections, $103 million to buy new voting machines, and $21 million to support voting audits following the election. But the Brennan Center's Lawrence Norden and Andrea Córdova McCadney insist more spending is needed. "As we noted when the grants were issued," say Norden and Córdova McCadney, "the way the money was distributed means it was insufficient to replace the vast majority of the most vulnerable machines before the 2020 election."[37] Norden and Córdova McCadney report that 121 election officials in thirty-one states say they urgently need to replace voting equipment before the next election in 2020. Most of these machines are no longer in production and are nearly impossible to service with spare parts. Moreover, spending money on repairs simply props up an outdated system. Yet two-thirds of officials say the additional HAVA funds they have received are still not enough to purchase new machines.

Scrutiny on Makers of Voting Machines

Concerns about the security of voting machines has brought new questions about the companies that manufacture and sell them. These companies, serving a limited market mostly in North America, maintain a near monopoly on election-related items such as voting machines. According to Marian Schneider, president of Verified Voting, a group that promotes election security practices, "I don't think the for-profit commercial model works particularly well for voting systems, because there's not enough profit in them to do really good R&D [research and development]."[38] Competition among the companies is fierce. Experts say this leads to secretiveness and reluctance to admit errors that can influence elections. The companies are willing to go to court to prevent their patented software from being examined, even after glitches are acknowledged.

Failures in cybersecurity are often kept hidden. The Mueller Report claims that Russians breached the computers of at least one voting machine maker (the name of which was redacted) and managed to infect the company's network with malware, information that had not previously been made public. Before it exited the business, Diebold was found to have left the source code for its machines on an unprotected server. To safeguard American

Americans Are Concerned About Election Interference

Large numbers of Americans say they are extremely or very concerned about foreign interference in the 2020 presidential election. This is the finding of a June 2019 poll by the Associated Press news service and the NORC Center for Public Affairs Research at the University of Chicago. Fifty percent of those polled describe themselves as either extremely or very concerned that foreign governments will tamper with voting systems or election results. This contrasts with 21 percent who say they are not very or not at all concerned with vote tampering. Other big concerns involve the theft of information from candidates or political parties and foreign influence on candidates and voters.

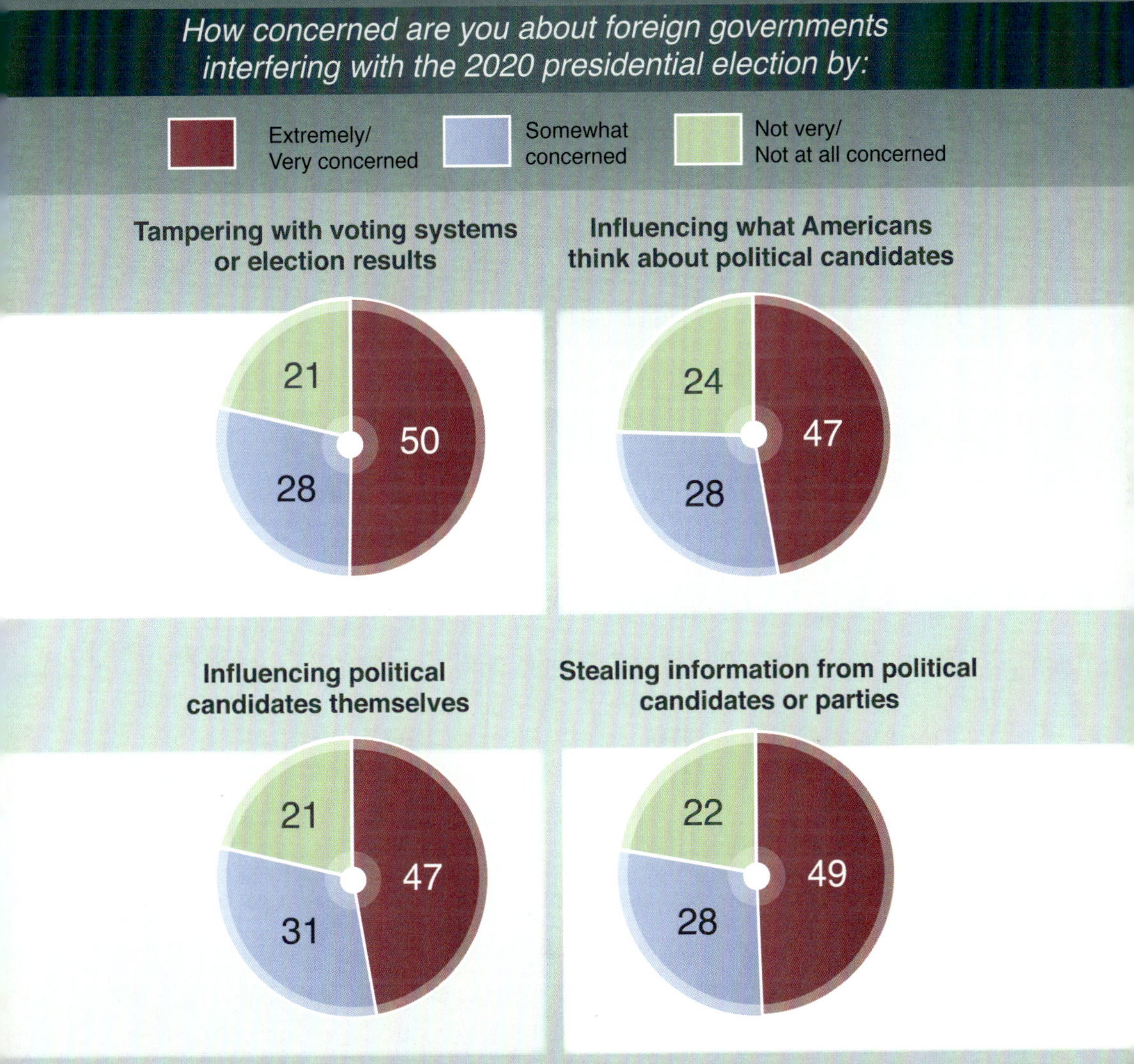

Source: Associated Press-NORC Center for Public Affairs Research, "AP-NORC Center Poll," June 2019. www.apnorc.org.

democracy, some analysts insist that election-related companies should be subject to more background checks and government regulation.

About 80 percent of America's voting machines are manufactured or serviced by three companies: Dominion Voting Systems, a Canadian company; Election Systems & Software; and Hart InterCivic. Other firms, like the Spanish company Scytl, provide election-related services, such as vote reporting and auditing tools. A proposed bill by Maryland representative Jamie Raskin would prevent foreign-owned companies from contracting with states for election management. Raskin has reason to be wary of foreign influence among voting machine makers. In 2018 the FBI notified Maryland officials that its main supplier of voting machines had been acquired by a parent company linked to a notorious Russian oligarch. Although the feds found no signs of vote tampering in Maryland, the opportunity for Russian influence threw up a red flag. "To say that they don't have any evidence of any wrongdoing is not to say that nothing untoward happened," says Raskin. "It's simply to say that we don't have the evidence of it."[39] The supplier, which is still doing business with Maryland election boards, is no longer owned by the Russian firm.

Hacking Vote-Reporting Networks

One part of the voting system may be more vulnerable to hacking than voting machines or voter registration lists. As one former senior intelligence official says, "If I was going to hack such a system, I'd leave the records alone and corrupt the tally software."[40] These software programs count the votes and send the results to a county election board or some other central site. The network over which the vote tally is transmitted presents a ripe opportunity for hackers. Some systems transmit unofficial vote totals via USB ports, which also pose little resistance to hackers. It is possible that hackers could use these access routes to slip malicious code into the system for sabotage at a later date. As *New York Times* reporter Kim Zetter explains:

Attackers could design their code to bypass pre-election testing and kick in only at the end of an election or under specific conditions—say, when a certain candidate appears to be losing—and erase itself afterward to avoid detection. And they could make it produce election results with wide margins to avoid triggering automatic manual recounts in states that require them when results are close.[41]

Systems also become open to this kind of attack when manufacturers leave their own servers unsecured. In 2017 an unprotected server at Election Systems & Software left passwords for its programmer exposed. These programmers create files that

A Diebold voting machine sits on display at the Def Con Hacking Conference in Las Vegas, Nevada. Before it left the voting system business, Diebold was found to have left the source code for its machines on an unprotected server.

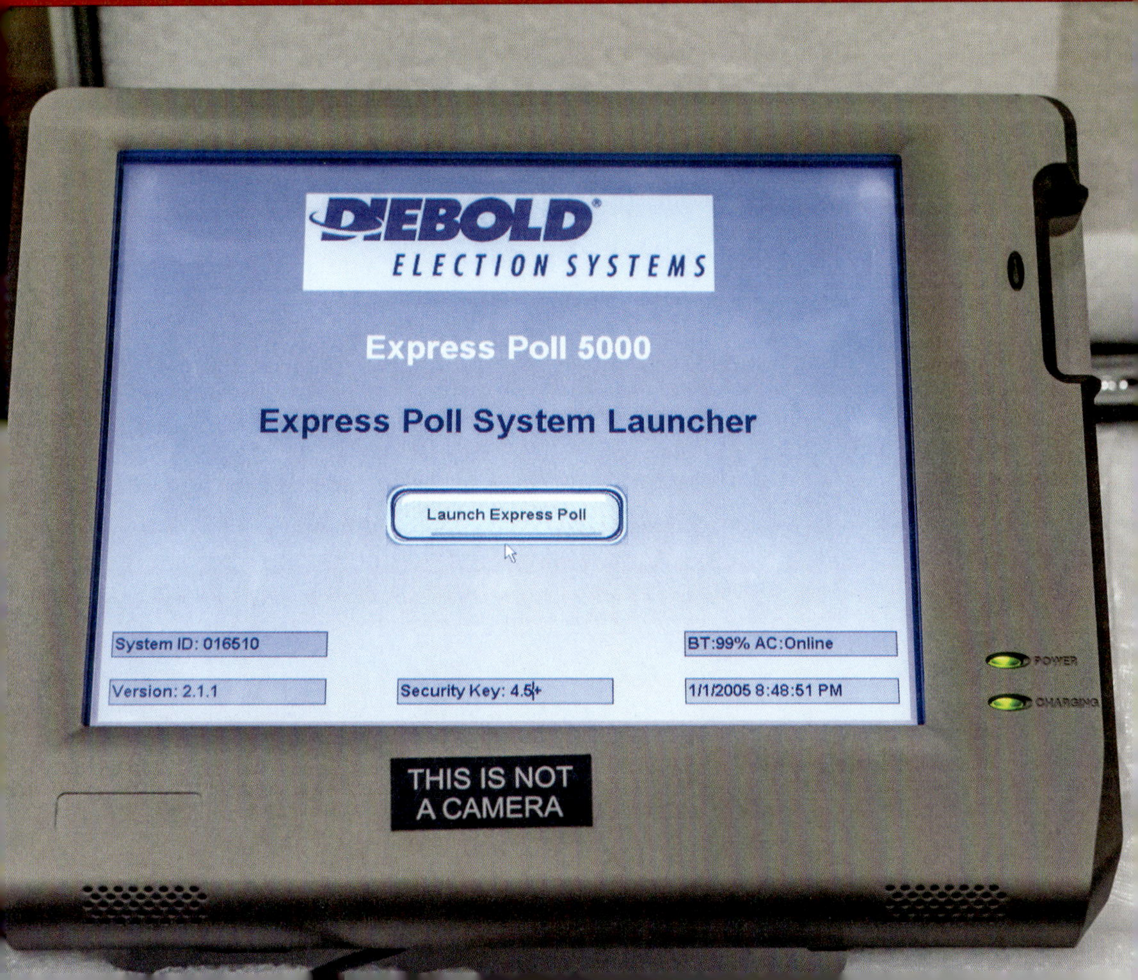

tell machines how to distribute votes based on touch screen or paper ballot voting. Using the passwords, hackers could reprogram the machines to interpret a vote for one candidate as a vote for his or her opponent. Knowing that these methods of sabotaging the vote are possible—whether or not they have actually been used—raises doubts about election results and eats away at public trust in the voting system. For Russians or other foreign hackers, creating a cloud of suspicion may be their main objective from the start.

Despite assurances from election officials that voting machines are secure, hackers have demonstrated they can be breached and compromised. Security experts say election boards across the country need to replace outdated machines and move to ma-

A New Plan for Online Voting

Online voting was once considered the ideal solution for future elections. That was before the public learned about the full capabilities of malicious hackers. Today experts agree that voting online is dangerously insecure. They say it invites fraud and enables hackers to link to voter databases, delete votes, or vote multiple times.

Nonetheless, one form of online voting is still being used in many states—for absentee ballots. An absentee ballot is one cast by a voter who is unable to go to a polling place. Most absentee ballots come from overseas. They are cast by US citizens serving in the military or living or working in a foreign country. In nineteen states and the District of Columbia, voters are allowed to cast absentee ballots by email or fax. In 2018 West Virginia made a mobile app available for military and overseas voters. The app uses blockchain, an encryption technology, to secure the transmission of ballots. Although election experts are skeptical about blockchain, West Virginia officials plan to expand the program for the 2020 election. "We are not saying mobile voting is the best solution to the problem, we are not saying that blockchain technology is the best solution to storage of security data," admits Donald Kersey, West Virginia's elections director. "What we are saying though is that it's better than what we have."

Quoted in Mike Orcutt, "West Virginia Will Allow 'Blockchain Voting' in the 2020 Election. That's a Risky Idea," *MIT Technology Review*, April 18, 2019. www.technologyreview.com.

chines with paper backup to protect the integrity of the vote. Not only do older voting machines malfunction more often, they also present easy targets for hackers. Many experts also urge more scrutiny on the handful of companies that manufacture and service voting machines. Even vote-reporting systems are vulnerable to hacking and sabotage. "In the fullness of time, a major election will be stolen by a nation-state cyber attack unless we improve the technology," says Halderman, the University of Michigan election security expert. "It's just too tempting a target, and too easy to get away with."[42]

"In the fullness of time, a major election will be stolen by a nation-state cyber attack unless we improve the technology."[42]

—J. Alex Halderman, a computer scientist and election security expert at the University of Michigan

The Future of Election Security

Federal bureaucrats usually know which agency to consult to address any emergency—but not always. In 2016 federal investigators learned that hackers had breached election board computers in Illinois and Arizona. Neil Jenkins, a director in the Office of Cybersecurity and Communications at the DHS, realized it might be the work of the same Russian hackers who had stolen files from the DNC and the Clinton campaign. Jenkins decided that state and local election officials across the nation needed to be notified at once. However, reaching out individually to more than ten thousand US election jurisdictions would take too long. One of Jenkins's aides suggested enlisting the FEC—but another staff member recalled that the FEC handles campaign finance, not election security. It took a Google search to determine that election-related issues were the responsibility of the US Election Assistance Commission (EAC). The EAC serves, quietly, as an advisory board for those thousands of state election officials. "I'm embarrassed to admit I didn't know that the EAC existed," Jenkins told the *New York Times*. "I would say that I'm not the only person working in the federal government that this was true for. This topic is not something that was really on anybody's big radar."[43]

A Challenge for the EAC

Since then, things have changed utterly. With all the revelations about Russian hacking, election security looms as one of the most important issues in America. Experts are urging the US government to be more aggressive in promoting the security and integrity of the nation's elections. They also want the president to take a strong stand against foreign governments that might seek to tamper with the 2020 presidential election. However, Trump has mostly rejected concerns about foreign election interference. As he told White House reporters on May 31, 2019, "No, Russia did not help me get elected."[44]

According to many political analysts, Trump refuses to acknowledge the Russian threat to US elections because he believes it casts doubt on his legitimacy as president. Furthermore, people in his administration follow his lead. "Every person who works for a presidential administration—Democrat or Republican—is aware of what the President's priorities are, what he cares about and what he doesn't," says Chris Cillizza, a political analyst at CNN. "[The administration] ignores—or slow-plays—issues that it knows the President either doesn't care about or for which he has actively expressed disdain."[45] Because of Trump's comments, Cillizza believes election security is not a priority for the Trump White House.

"[The administration] ignores—or slow-plays—issues that it knows the President either doesn't care about or for which he has actively expressed disdain."[45]

—Chris Cillizza, a political analyst at CNN

In this atmosphere, dealing with election security issues is a challenge for staffers at the EAC. The agency was created in 2002 as part of the Help America Vote Act. Its mission to oversee the election process nationwide has seen mixed results. The EAC's budget has been cut from $17 million in 2009 to $10 million today. Its staff has shrunk from fifty full-time employees to barely more than twenty. Only a handful of its employees still work on one of its core duties, which is the testing and certification of voting machines. At a May 21, 2019, congressional hearing, Christy McCormick, one of four EAC commissioners, raised concerns about funding and personnel. She admitted that her staff was strained to the breaking point trying to keep up with the demands of machine testing. According to McCormick, the agency is desperately in need of more money. Adding to the crunch, two different directors of testing and certification at the EAC stepped down in the first half of 2019.

The EAC has its own critics. State and local election officials have complained about EAC leadership and its lax approach to shoring up election systems. State officials say the EAC has failed to follow through on security training, leaving them to rely on the DHS, which lacks experience in some of the current issues surrounding voting systems. Some say that Republicans in the EAC leadership tend to downplay the threat to secure voting. One EAC commissioner reportedly told local officials that concerns about foreign meddling in US elections were overblown. Brian Newby,

Some political analysts believe President Trump refuses to acknowledge the Russian threat to US elections because he is afraid it casts doubt on the legitimacy of his presidency.

the EAC's executive director, has come under fire for what some in Congress feel is a lackluster performance. Staff members say Newby has blocked them from preparing the guidance materials that are vital for state and local election officials. Newby also has called off staff member trips to state offices for conferences or training sessions in election security. "This is really the moment that the EAC should be much more high-profile, and they're missing the opportunity," says one election expert. "As we're going into 2020, this is the time where they should be getting that attention, and there is no plan for that."[46]

Federal Versus State Oversight of Elections

Federal oversight of election security is limited. This is because traditionally, elections in the United States are under state and local control. The July 2019 Senate Intelligence Committee report on Russian election interference claims that hackers have taken advantage of gaps between the election expertise of federal agencies and the uneven security efforts of state and local election boards. Yet many state officials are wary of federal encroachment. Several years ago, Jeh Johnson, then-secretary of homeland security, suggested designating the nation's election system as so-called critical infrastructure—that is, a basic building block of American society. This would allow for more federal funding for election boards across the country. However, some state officials balked at what they feared might be a federal takeover of the election process.

Experts insist that election security is a national issue. They say Congress must act to ensure that voters in every state receive the same basic protections. "There is no question that the authority resides with the states, but Congress not only has the right but an obligation to make sure federal elections are secure," says Lawrence Norden of the Brennan Center for Justice. "There is a place for Congress to say that we want all Americans to trust in our elections and there are minimum standards that everyone should abide by."[47]

Going further, some analysts believe the state-run election system is hopelessly outdated and should be scrapped in favor of federal control. But even those who are sympathetic to the idea see too many practical problems for such a sweeping change. The cost, in both time and money, of installing standardized voting equipment and setting up new protocols at polling places would be enormous. "If we were to federalize elections, we're not just going to flip a switch on that," notes David Becker, founder of the Center for Election Innovation & Research. "It would be a long-term, really expensive solution and it would create a new bureaucracy."[48]

> **"If we were to federalize elections, we're not just going to flip a switch on that. It would be a long-term, really expensive solution and it would create a new bureaucracy."[48]**
>
> —David Becker, founder of the Center for Election Innovation & Research

Resistance to Federal Control of Elections

In March 2018, with mounting evidence of Russian meddling in US elections, there seemed to be bipartisan support for election security. As part of a massive spending bill, Congress included $380 million for states to replace aging voting machines, set up postelection audits, and provide training in cybersecurity. An additional $300 million went to the FBI to counter hacking attempts. Security experts agreed the spending was a step in the right direction, but they stressed the need for much more. In 2019 the Democrat-controlled House passed an election security bill that required all polling places to have paper backups for electronic voting machines. The bill received only one Republican vote. In the Senate, Republican majority leader Mitch McConnell blocked the bill, along with other election reform efforts that would funnel more than $1 billion to state and local officials to beef up ballot box security. This prompted McConnell's opponents to call him "Moscow Mitch" and accuse him of going soft on Russian election tampering. In September 2019, McConnell did announce his support for $250 million in funding for election security, an amount his critics derided as far too meager.

Republicans like McConnell are against handing over control of elections to the federal government. They consider state and local election boards fully capable of conducting elections with a

Republicans like Mitch McConnell (pictured) are against handing over control of elections to the federal government. They consider state and local election boards to be capable of managing the process.

minimum of federal oversight. Imposing a one-size-fits-all solution, they believe, could actually stifle innovation at the state level instead of boosting it. Moreover, conservatives point to some security analysts who say the decentralized nature of the US voting system actually makes it more difficult to hack.

Developing New Election Systems

Some states and counties are developing their own election systems to increase security. Los Angeles County, the nation's largest voting jurisdiction with 5.2 million residents, is launching Voting Solutions for All People (VSAP). The huge $300 million project has been in the planning stages for a decade. VSAP

State Spending on Election Security

Despite worries about potential foreign interference in the 2020 elections, states seem in no hurry to spend federal funds on election security. On April 4, 2019, the EAC reported that just 8 percent of $380 million in federal grants had been spent in the first six months after the funds were distributed. More than half of the $31.4 million spent by states went to cybersecurity. This included adding new workers to assess risks and vulnerabilities in networks and shoring up firewalls for statewide voter registration databases. Rhode Island acquired a new coded platform for its database. Delaware spent most of its $3 million grant for a down payment on new voting machines. Colorado, Iowa, and New Jersey paid for exercises that simulate cyberattacks on election offices.

The EAC hopes that most of the grant money can be distributed before the 2020 election. A majority of spending goes toward subgrants to individual counties and districts. Smaller counties are seeking to increase security for electronic poll books, systems that report election-night results, and voter information websites. Many states are also continuing to replace outdated voting machines, a task that costs much more than the grant money available. EAC officials also say replacing machines takes up to a year. As Mark Abbott, the EAC's commission grants director, notes, "If they haven't started the procurement process, it's unlikely new equipment will be in place by 2020."

Quoted in Benjamin Freed, "States' Spending on Election Security Expected to Pick Up in 2019," Statescoop, April 4, 2019. www.statescoop.com.

will introduce new voting machines and a new system for voting just in time for the presidential primary in March 2020. Instead of casting their ballots at traditional polling places on Election Day, voters in Los Angeles County will have up to eleven days to vote at any of the new voting centers set up throughout the county.

The voting centers will be equipped with thirty-one thousand new ballot-marking devices that county officials claim are the latest in election security. Voters make their selections on a touch screen and then print out a paper summary to check. The printout is fed back into a secure box attached to the machine. Staffers at each voting center will be available to help those voters who are less tech-savvy. Voters will also have the option to prepare a sample ballot on their own tablet or cell phone to make the process easier. The centers are designed to facilitate voting for the disabled and non-English-speakers as well. Overall, county elections chief Dean Logan hopes to win the confidence of voters with voting centers that are comfortable yet secure. "His vision has always been to create a new voting system," says Marilu Guevara, executive director of the League of Women Voters of Los Angeles. "He would have people voting at Starbucks, if he could find a responsible and secure way to do it."[49]

Nonetheless, the VSAP project has not lacked controversy. Smartmatic, the multinational elections company teaming with Los Angeles County on VSAP, has drawn inquiries about its foreign connections, particularly its origins in Venezuela under Hugo Chávez, the now deceased dictator. Alleged glitches in Smartmatic machines have led to protests in the Philippines, Estonia, and other countries. Mindful of the threat of foreign influence in elections, critics have questioned whether Smartmatic was a wise choice as a partner on VSAP. However, Logan thinks the concern is misplaced. "They're building the equipment based on our design, our blueprints, our plans," he says. "And at the end of the

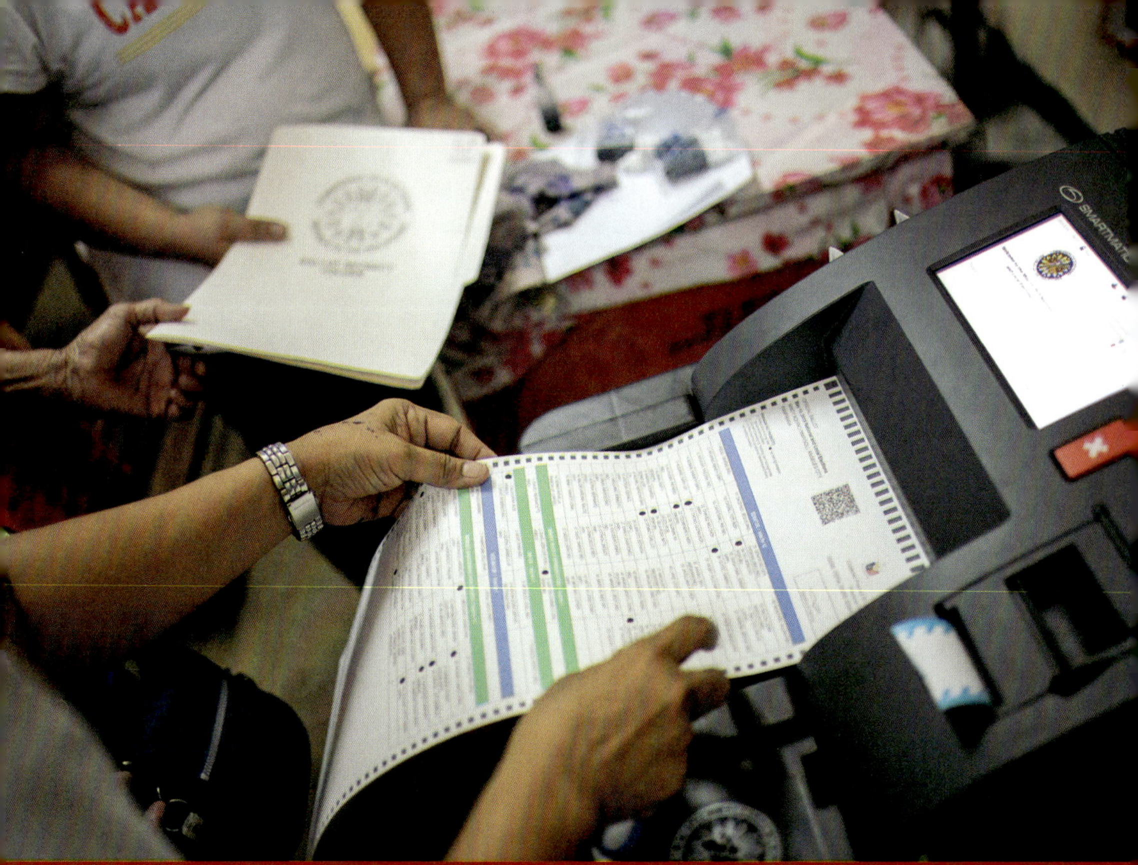

Smartmatic voting machines (pictured) have been suspected of malfunctioning in elections. Due to the company's foreign connections, critics have questioned whether Smartmatic was a wise choice as a partner for the VSAP project in Los Angeles County.

day, once that equipment is built and the system exists, it will belong to L.A. County. Smartmatic won't be running our elections."[50]

Risk-Limiting Audits

Election officials like Logan are always in search of new ways to bolster the election process and inspire confidence in voters. This has led to districts retiring old voting machines and mandating a paper trail to audit results. Another new procedure that can provide confidence in election results is the risk-limiting audit (RLA). The Brennan Center for Justice considers this measure crucial to making elections more secure and defending against hacks. According to the Brennan Center's Andrea Córdova McCadney, Elizabeth Howard, and Lawrence Norden, "RLAs can provide assurance that the reported winner did, in fact, win the election, instead of a traditional audit, which only assures officials that machines are working correctly."[51] Some states have already used their share of federal funds for election improvements to test and implement RLAs.

The idea behind the RLA is to use statistics and manual paper audits to ensure that the correct candidate is declared the winner. In traditional audits, a set percentage of ballots are counted to check whether the results make sense. By contrast, an RLA is based on the margin of victory and the total number of ballots cast. In an RLA, the number of ballots counted depends on the closeness of the race. If the race is very close, a larger sample of ballots is counted. RLAs help officials spot discrepancies in

End-to-End Verifiable Voting

Computer scientists have developed a tweak to voting systems that helps each voter check that his or her vote is recorded accurately. The technology is called end-to-end verifiable voting, or E2E-V for short. With E2E-V, a voter casts a vote by touch screen in the usual way and receives two paper printouts. One is a readable summary of the voter's choices, along with a random serial number. The other is a receipt with a twenty-character code that locks in the voter's choices and serial number. Meanwhile, the voting terminal encrypts, or places into code, the voter's ballot and stores it in its memory. The ballot is then linked to the serial number and the code.

Using the E2E-V system, each voter has a way to verify that the machine is not malfunctioning or cheating. A voter can choose to create a so-called spoiled ballot—sort of a practice ballot. This is a random ballot produced on the touch screen to check that the encryption is accurate. Once the voter is satisfied that the system is working properly, he or she can then cast the real vote. Computer scientists say that testing a certain number of spoiled ballots ensures that mismarked or miscounted ballots will be detected immediately. A major drawback, however, is understanding how E2E-V works. "Myself, I am not convinced that E2E-Verifiable voting is understandable enough to voters, to election administrators, to the public," says computer scientist Andrew Appel. "If people can't understand something, how can they trust it?"

Andrew Appel, "End-to-End Verifiable Elections," *Freedom to Tinker* (blog), September 19, 2019. www.freedom-to-tinker.com.

vote totals—for example, from voting machine malfunctions or hacking attempts—that otherwise might be missed. Statisticians, political scientists, and voting security experts have all praised RLAs as an important step forward in election security. And states are embracing the idea. Colorado performed a statewide RLA in the 2018 election, while other states are either adopting RLAs by law or running test programs for 2020.

> **"RLAs can provide assurance that the reported winner did, in fact, win the election, instead of a traditional audit, which only assures officials that machines are working correctly."[51]**
>
> —Andrea Córdova McCadney, Elizabeth Howard, and Lawrence Norden of the Brennan Center for Justice

Trump appears reluctant to address the issue of election interference. Lack of White House support makes it more difficult for agencies like the EAC to help state and county election boards safeguard the voting process. Democrats favor federal oversight of elections, while Republicans prefer the tradition of state and local control. Election boards across the nation are retiring old voting machines and going to paper backups for audits in order to protect against hacking attempts and tampering. Some districts are rethinking the whole voting process. New ideas like RLAs can also help bolster confidence in election outcomes. Experts say more innovations are needed to secure US elections from interference in the future.

Introduction: A Stern Warning

1. Quoted in Julie Hirschfeld and Mark Mazzetti, "Highlights of Robert Mueller's Testimony to Congress," *New York Times*, July 24, 2019. www.nytimes.com.
2. Quoted in Julian E. Barnes and Adam Goldman, "F.B.I. Warns of Russian Interference in 2020 Race and Boosts Counterintelligence Operations," *New York Times*, April 26, 2019. www.nytimes.com.
3. Quoted in Tim Lau, "U.S. Elections Are Still Vulnerable to Foreign Hacking," Brennan Center for Justice, July 18, 2019. www.brennancenter.org.

Chapter One: Hacking into Campaign Networks

4. Quoted in Nat Levy, "Microsoft Warns of Increased Attacks Ahead of European Elections, Expands AccountGuard Cybersecurity Program," GeekWire, February 19, 2019. www.geekwire.com.
5. Brad Smith, "We Are Taking New Steps Against Broadening Threats to Democracy," *Microsoft on the Issues* (blog), August 20, 2018. http://blogs.microsoft.com.
6. Quoted in Dan Patterson, "How Microsoft's Defending Democracy Program Amplifies Account Security," TechRepublic, October 31, 2018. www.techrepublic.com.
7. Danielle Kurtzleben, "Here's How Many Bernie Sanders Supporters Ultimately Voted for Trump," NPR, August 24, 2017. www.npr.org.
8. Quoted in Eric Geller, "Collusion Aside, Mueller Found Abundant Evidence of Russian Election Plot," Politico, April 18, 2019. www.politico.com.
9. Quoted in Dustin Volz and Tarini Parti, "2020 Campaigns Remain Vulnerable as Signs of Russian Hackers Re-emerge," *Wall Street Journal*, June 13, 2019. www.wsj.com.

10. Quoted in Shannon Vavra, "FEC Allows Nonprofit to Provide Free Cybersecurity Services to Campaigns," CyberScoop, May 23, 2019. www.cyberscoop.com.
11. Quoted in Volz and Parti, "2020 Campaigns Remain Vulnerable as Signs of Russian Hackers Re-emerge."
12. Quoted in CBS News, "Password Security Tips to Help You Foil Hackers," March 17, 2017. www.cbsnews.com.
13. Quoted in Zaid Shoorbajee, "Here Are All of the Election Security Offerings from Private Companies," CyberScoop, August 20, 2018. www.cyberscoop.com.

Chapter Two: Spreading Fake News on Social Media

14. Quoted in Nancy Scola, "FEC Chair Summons Facebook, Twitter, Google to Disinformation Session," *Politico*, August 29, 2019. www.politico.com.
15. Quoted in Taylor Lorenz, "Trump Has Changed How Teens View the News," *The Atlantic*, August 29, 2018. www.theatlantic.com.
16. Quoted in Mike Wendling, "The (Almost) Complete History of 'Fake News,'" BBC, January 22, 2018. www.bbc.com.
17. Quoted in Ryan Broderick, "Here's Everything the Mueller Report Says About How Russian Trolls Used Social Media," BuzzFeed, April 18, 2019. www.buzzfeednews.com.
18. Josh Constine, "Trump and Clinton Spent $81M on US Election Facebook Ads, Russian Agency $46K," TechCrunch, November 1, 2017. http://techcrunch.com.
19. Quoted in Danielle Kurtzleben, "Did Fake News on Facebook Help Elect Trump? Here's What We Know," NPR, April 11, 2018. www.npr.org.
20. Quoted in Rob Matheson, "Peering Under the Hood of Fake-News Detectors," MIT News, February 6, 2019. http://news.mit.edu.
21. Quoted in CBS News, "Doctored Nancy Pelosi Video Highlights Threat of 'Deepfake' Tech," May 25, 2019. www.cbsnews.com.

22. Quoted in Khari Johnson, "Deepfake Concerns Ahead of 2020 Election Include Iran, China, Instagram, and WhatsApp," VentureBeat, September 3, 2019. www.venturebeat.com.
23. Quoted in Johnson, "Deepfake Concerns Ahead of 2020 Election Include Iran, China, Instagram, and WhatsApp."

Chapter Three: Tampering with Voter Databases

24. Quoted in Michael Wines, "Russians Breached Florida County Computers Before 2016 Election, Mueller Report Says," *New York Times*, April 18, 2019. www.nytimes.com.
25. Quoted in Frances Robles, "Russia Hackers Were 'in a Position' to Alter Florida Voter Rolls, Rubio Confirms," *New York Times*, April 26, 2019. www.nytimes.com.
26. Quoted in Tal Axelrod, "Rubio Says Hackers Penetrated Florida Elections Systems," *The Hill* (Washington, DC), April 26, 2019. www.thehill.com.
27. Charles P. Pierce, "We're Supposed to Believe the Russians Hacked into Voting Systems but Did Nothing Once They Got There?," *Esquire*, July 26, 2019. www.esquire.com.
28. Monica Pal, "Are Citizens Compromising Their Privacy When Registering to Vote?," GCN, December 11, 2018. www.gcn.com.
29. Quoted in Associated Press, "The Many State Election Systems Complicate Efforts to Stop Hackers," *Los Angeles Times*, July 28, 2019. www.latimes.com.
30. Quoted in P.K. Gray, "What States Are Getting Right—and Wrong—About Election Security," *Election Security* (blog), Symantec, March 21, 2019. www.symantec.com.
31. Quoted in Gray, "What States Are Getting Right—and Wrong—About Election Security."
32. Quoted in Laura Hautala, "States Brace for Ransomware Assaults on Voter Registries," CNET, September 1, 2019. www.cnet.com.

Chapter Four: Interfering with the Voting Process

33. Quoted in Igor Derysh, "Hackers Can Easily Break into Voting Machines Used Across the U.S.; Play *Doom*, *Nirvana*," Salon, August 14, 2019. www.salon.com.
34. Quoted in Derysh, "Hackers Can Easily Break into Voting Machines Used Across the U.S.; Play *Doom*, *Nirvana*."
35. Quoted in David E. Sanger and Catie Edmondson, "Russia Targeted Election Systems in All 50 States, Report Finds," *New York Times*, July 25, 2019. www.nytimes.com.
36. Tom Burt, "A Paper Record for Every Voter: It's Time for Congress to Act," Roll Call, June 7, 2019. www.rollcall.com.
37. Lawrence Norden and Andrea Córdova McCadney, "Voting Machines at Risk: Where We Stand Today," Brennan Center for Justice, March 5, 2019. www.brennancenter.org.
38. Quoted in Lily Hay Newman, "Election Security Is Still Hurting at Every Level," *Wired*, June 6, 2019. www.wired.com.
39. Quoted in Jordan Wilkie, "'They Think They Are Above the Law': The Firms That Own America's Voting System," *Guardian* (Manchester, UK), April 23, 2019. www.theguardian.com.
40. Quoted in Fred Kaplan, "Bring Back Paper Ballots," Slate, July 26, 2019. www.slate.com.
41. Kim Zetter, "The Crisis of Election Security," *New York Times Magazine*, September 26, 2018. www.nytimes.com.
42. Quoted in Sean Flynn, "How to Hack an Election," *GQ*, November 5, 2018. www.gq.com.

Chapter Five: The Future of Election Security

43. Quoted in Zetter, "The Crisis of Election Security."
44. Quoted in John Bowden, "Trump's Evolving Remarks on Russian Election Interference," *The Hill* (Washington, DC), June 1, 2019. www.thehill.com.
45. Chris Cillizza, "Don't Tell Donald Trump About Russia's Election Interference!," CNN, April 24, 2019. www.cnn.com.

46. Quoted in Eric Geller, "Federal Election Official Accused of Undermining His Own Agency," *Politico*, June 15, 2019. www.politico.com.
47. Quoted in Associated Press, "The Many State Election Systems Complicate Efforts to Stop Hackers."
48. Quoted in Associated Press, "The Many State Election Systems Complicate Efforts to Stop Hackers."
49. Quoted in Matt Stiles, "Sweeping Change Is Coming for L.A. County Voters. If Things Go Wrong, He'll Get the Blame," *Los Angeles Times*, August 19, 2019. www.latimes.com.
50. Quoted in Saul Gonzalez, "The Company Behind LA's New Election Infrastructure," KCRW, October 5, 2018. www.kcrw.com.
51. Andrea Córdova McCadney, Elizabeth Howard, and Lawrence Norden, "Voting Machine Security: Where We Stand Six Months Before the New Hampshire Primary," Brennan Center for Justice, August 12, 2019. www.brennancenter.org.

FOR FURTHER RESEARCH

Books

Jake Braun, *Democracy in Danger: How Hackers and Activists Exposed Fatal Flaws in the Election System*. Lanham, MD: Rowman & Littlefield, 2019.

Mitchell Brown, ed., *The Future of Election Administration: Elections, Voting, Technology*. New York: Palgrave Macmillan, 2019.

James W. Cortada and William Aspray, *Fake News Nation: The Long History of Lies and Misinterpretations in America*. Lanham, MD: Rowman & Littlefield, 2019.

Malcolm Nance, *The Plot to Hack America: How Putin's Cyberspies and WikiLeaks Tried to Steal the 2016 Election*. New York: Skyhorse, 2017.

Clint Watts, *Messing with the Enemy: Surviving in a Social Media World of Hackers, Terrorists, Russians, and Fake News*. New York: Harper Paperbacks, 2019.

Internet Sources

Joe Andrews, "Fake News Is Real—A.I. Is Going to Make It Much Worse," CNBC, July 12, 2019. www.cnbc.com.

Lawrence Norden and Andrea Córdova McCadney, "Voting Machines at Risk: Where We Stand Today," Brennan Center for Justice, March 5, 2019. www.brennancenter.org.

Nicole Perlroth and Matthew Rosenberg, "Election Rules Are an Obstacle to Cybersecurity of Presidential Campaigns," *New York Times*, June 6, 2019. www.nytimes.com.

Dustin Volz and Tarini Parti, "2020 Campaigns Remain Vulnerable as Signs of Russian Hackers Re-emerge," *Wall Street Journal*, June 13, 2019. www.wsj.com.

Kim Zetter, "The Crisis of Election Security," *New York Times Magazine*, September 26, 2018. www.nytimes.com.

Websites

Brookings Institution — www.brookings.edu

The Brookings Institution is a nonprofit public policy organization based in Washington, DC. Its mission is to conduct and present in-depth research on ideas for solving societal problems on the local, national, and international level. Among the articles on the Brookings website is "Political Campaigns Are the First Line of Defense in Election Security."

Defending Digital Democracy — www.belfercenter.org/project/defending-digital-democracy)

The Defending Digital Democracy Project at Harvard's Kennedy School of Government aims to develop strategies, tools, and technology to protect democratic processes and systems from cyber and information attacks. The project's bipartisan team of technology experts and leaders in cybersecurity are working to offer concrete solutions to the urgent problem of election hacking.

US Department of Justice — www.justice.gov/storage/report.pdf

Volumes I and II of the *Report on the Investigation into Russian Interference in the 2016 Presidential Election* by Special Counsel Robert S. Mueller III can be found here. The redacted report, released in March 2019 by the special counsel's office, appears in full. Related court documents, including indictments and plea agreements stemming from the investigation, can be found at www.justice.gov/sco.

US Election Assistance Commission — www.eac.gov

Created under the 2002 Help America Vote Act (HAVA), the EAC serves as a vital resource for administering elections in the United States. The EAC distributes federal funds to states, helps local election boards meet HAVA requirements, and conducts tests on and certifies voting equipment.

INDEX

Note: Boldface page numbers indicate illustrations.

PICTURE CREDITS

Cover: Jon Schulte/Shutterstock

6: Associated Press
10: VDB Photos/Shutterstock.com
13: Joseph Sohm/Shutterstock.com
17: OlhaYefimova/Shutterstock.com
22: Tero Vesalainen/Shutterstock.com
26: Associated Press
29: Sheila Fitzgerald/Shutterstock.com
33: Rob Crandall/Shutterstock.com
35: Alessandro Pietri/Shutterstock.com
42: Associated Press
46: Reuters/Newscom
51: Maury Aaseng
53: Bing Wen/Shutterstock.com
58: Michael Candelori/Shutterstock.com
61: Christopher Halloran/Shutterstock.com
64: Dave Tacon/Polaris/Newscom

ABOUT THE AUTHOR

John Allen is a writer who lives in Oklahoma City.

WITHDRAWN